mettle

BIBLE READING NOTES

TO INSPIRE
COURAGE
SPIRIT
CHARACTER

yfc   CWR

MIX
Paper from
responsible sources
FSC® C015900

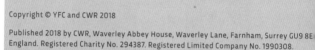

CONTENTS

Welcome to

mettle

COURAGE SPIRIT CHARACTER...

Welcome to a new issue *Mettle* for the summer months! We hope you enjoy this issue of notes and draw closer to God and His Word.

The core theme for the next few months is creation. If you have watched the *Blue Planet* or *Planet Earth* programmes, you will know that the world is an incredible place. But what does that tell us about the creator God who made it?

Then our three hot topics – dating, money and apologetics – are challenging but important subjects. Does God gives us any guidance about our relationships? What should be our attitude to money? How can we give confident and coherent answers to those who question us about our faith?

We hope and pray that these notes will be a practical aid for your walk with God!

The *Mettle* Team

TUES 1 MAY

CREATION

Creator God

READ: GENESIS 1:1–13

KEY VERSE V1
'In the beginning God created'

Let's start at the very beginning. A very good place to start according to Maria in *The Sound of Music*. So what better place to begin our series on 'Creation', than right at the beginning of everything? The very first time the Bible mentions God, what is He doing? He's creating – making stuff. He's not judging people, getting angry or giving long lists of commandments. He's doing something incredible: making something out of nothing. The first thing the Bible tells us about God is that He's a creator. He brings order out of chaos; He brings shape and colour out of darkness and emptiness; He brings life out of nothing.

If we look at the world around us, we can see how amazingly detailed and beautiful and vibrant it is. A flea can jump 150 times its own length and pull 160,000 times its own weight. The human eye can see up to 10 million different colours and 5 trillion hydrogen atoms can fit onto a pinhead. It's absolutely astonishing! It would be difficult to believe that a world like this simply 'happened'. The world is so amazing and wonderful because God made it, and *He* is wonderful. It's in His nature to be creative, innovative and surprising, and He hasn't changed – He's still all of these things today.

Over the next few days, we'll be learning more about the wonderful world around us and what it can tell us about the God who made it. We'll also be thinking about our responsibilities to look after God's world. But, for now, just think about this...

Think

The same God who created the world and made it amazing is with us right now. What's more, He's interested in what's going on in our lives. Let's tell Him now how much we appreciate Him.

Stars in outer space

≡ **READ: GENESIS 1:14–19**

KEY VERSE V16
'He also made the stars.'

CORE THEME | CREATION

→ In the middle of God creating light, sky, land and sea, the sun and moon, trees and plants, there's a sentence in Genesis 1 – almost a throwaway comment – that could easily be overlooked. 'He also made the stars' (v16). It makes it sound as if this was an easy, almost insignificant thing for God to do! It is impossible to know for sure the number of stars there are in the whole universe but suffice it to say there are a lot – too many to count.

Space is huge, *really* huge. The nearest star to earth (apart from our own sun) is Proxima Centauri. And Proxima Centauri is 4.25 light years away. So even if you travelled at the speed of light, it would still take you more than four years to get there! Or, to put it another way, imagine a '4' with thirteen '0's after it, and that's approximately the number of kilometres between earth and the nearest star other than the sun. The earth's own galaxy is just one of millions of galaxies in the universe. The numbers and the distances involved are mind-boggling. Space is absolutely vast. And God created it!

➕ ## Challenge

Look up some facts about the universe. Visit a few websites, and learn about some different stars and constellations. Find out what a black hole is or what happens when a star dies. Why not borrow a telescope and see what can be seen on a clear night?

Incredible imagination

READ: GENESIS 1:20–25

KEY VERSE V24
'Let the land produce living creatures according to their kinds'

Scientists have discovered approximately 950,000 species of insects, all of which are slightly different. What's more, it's thought that there are still nearly nine million more species to discover. This is just the insects! To think that God went to the trouble of creating ten million different species of insects is just astounding.

There's immense diversity amongst the animals God created, too. So many animals are incredible, for all sorts of reasons – lions, for example, because they are so powerful. Then there are all those brightly coloured birds and fish. Hummingbirds have the 'wow' factor because of their ability to hover by beating their wings up to 90 times a second! Giraffes are amazing, funny-looking creatures, but they were designed that way so that they could reach to eat leaves from tall trees.

The huge variety of animals in the world is really impressive. There's a massive range of shapes, colours and abilities. If God created animals with that kind of diversity, He must be stunningly creative and have an incredible eye for detail. Who else but God would have thought to give the chameleon the ability to change colour?

CORE THEME | CREATION

➕ Challenge

Watch a wildlife documentary and take time to appreciate the diverse and wonderfully designed animal kingdom. Then praise God for being such an amazing creator.

Guardians of the planet

READ: GENESIS 1:26–30

KEY VERSE V28
'fill the earth and subdue it.'

Imagine your parents are out of town for the weekend. 'Brilliant!' you think, 'I have the place to myself!' So what might happen? You eat what you want from the fridge. You play your music at full volume. You push your little brother around. You invite all your friends round. You have a great time. When your parents get home, they find the fridge empty, the house a mess, your little brother in tears and the neighbours angry about all the noise.

God has put us in charge of the beautiful world He created. Some people misunderstand this and think that the world is ours, that we can do what we like with it and that the consequences don't matter. It's this kind of short-term thinking that leads to pollution, climate change and the extinction of more and more species of animals. For example, the adorable Adélie penguin is incredibly vulnerable to the consequences of climate change.

This really isn't what God had in mind. He put us in charge of creation to look after it. It's ours to take care of, but we don't own it – it's still God's. God created a beautiful world – and He's given us the responsibility to keep it that way.

Pray

Lord, I'm sorry for the times when I take the world for granted. Help me to remember that I have a responsibility to look after creation. Help me to see what I can do to keep the world beautiful. Amen.

CORE THEME | CREATION

Weekend

5/6 MAY

Mountaintop views

≡ **READ: GENESIS 1:31–2:3**

KEY VERSE 1:31
'God saw all that he had made, and it was very good.'

Have you ever visited Mount Snowdon, the highest mountain in Wales and England? It is climbed every year by 350,000 visitors, with many footpaths to cater for different levels of fitness. However, if you feel that walking up the mountain is beyond you, there is also a steam railway that will take you all the way up to the summit in the summer months. It is definitely worth the effort because the vista from the summit is breath-taking – in 2017 it was named the best view in the UK!

On a sunny day, Snowdon's summit, 3,560ft about sea level, offers stunning 360-degree views over the beautiful surrounding Welsh countryside and Llyn Llydaw, the long narrow lake beneath the Mount. If it's clear, you can see all the way to Ireland. The jaw-dropping vistas remind us how magnificent the world is, and how great God is.

It's funny how easy it is to take our world for granted. Often when we are passengers in cars, trains or buses, we spend the time looking down at our mobile devices instead of at the beautiful countryside just outside the window. But, every so often, at places like Snowdon, we're reminded of just how good the world is. Really, the wonders of our planet are impossible to ignore. The world God created is truly amazing! When we come to recognise that, our immediate response should be to praise God for what He's made. David was especially gifted at finding the right words to praise God. In the Psalms he says, 'Before the mountains were born or you brought forth the whole world, from everlasting to everlasting you are God' (Psa. 90:2).

 ## *Think*

Whatever you're doing and wherever you are going today, ask God to show you how good the world is. Then look up and around you. What can you see to thank God for?

Key ingredient

READ: COLOSSIANS 1:15–17

KEY VERSE V17
'He is before all things, and in him all things hold together.'

Have you ever tried making bread without flour? Or mixing cement without sand? Flour and sand are essential components – bread without flour would be a useless mess. A wall made without sand in the cement would fall down in no time. If we miss out a crucial part of something, we shouldn't really be surprised when that thing falls apart or doesn't turn out as planned.

Sometimes we may take for granted something fundamental like clean air, but as soon as it's missing or polluted, things start to go badly wrong and we feel the effects. When God created the world, He created it perfectly and set the laws of nature in place – day and night, the rising and setting sun, wind and rain. Even though, as a result of the Fall, sin has caused the perfection to be flawed in some ways, it is still Christ who holds all things together.

And it's Jesus who looks after us too. A lot of the time, we might not even be aware of what Jesus is doing, but we can be sure that if He wasn't there, everything around us would fall apart. There may be times when we take our relationship with Jesus for granted. Let's remember that He needs to be the key ingredient in our lives.

Pray

Jesus, You are the single most important person in all creation. Thank You for holding all things together, even when I can't see You at work. Amen.

CORE THEME | CREATION

Mission possible

READ: ROMANS 4:16–22

KEY VERSE V17
'God who gives life to the dead and calls into being things that were not.'

CORE THEME | CREATION

Nothing is impossible for God. Just ask Abraham! Put yourself in Abraham's place for a minute. God has promised you so many descendants that you won't be able to count them. But you're nearly 100 years old, your wife isn't getting any younger either, and so far you haven't managed to produce a single baby! In these circumstances, you'd be forgiven for wondering whether maybe God had forgotten about you. Did Abraham begin to think like that? We don't know for sure. But we do know that, deep down, he never stopped believing that God would keep His promise and give him a child. And that's exactly what happened.

Abraham knew that God was faithful, and he also knew that God could still work in seemingly impossible situations. The same is true today. Our God is Abraham's God: 'the God who gives life to the dead and calls into being things that were not'(v17). God can create something incredible out of nothing. God gave a couple of senior citizens a baby, and He can create awesome things in our lives too.

Think

Is there any area of your life where you've stopped believing that God can turn things around? Spend some time remembering occasions in the past when God has kept His promises and done brilliant stuff for you. Talk this over with a friend if it helps.

Designed by God

 READ: ROMANS 1:18–23

KEY VERSE V20
'For since the creation of the world God's invisible qualities – his eternal power and divine nature – have been clearly seen'

When you initially acquire a brilliant new phone, it looks really cool and is simple to use. You can download all your favourite music onto it, plus games and applications. The only problem is: it's difficult to leave the phone alone and do some work! But, however clever phones are, it's not the phone itself that's really impressive – it's the people who designed it.

Today's verses remind us that something similar is true about the world. It's an amazing place. We've already mentioned how intricate, detailed and beautiful it is. But we're missing the point if we admire the world itself and forget the God who put it together.

Everything in creation points us towards God. It's as though His fingerprints are all over it. Some people refuse to see that, which is sad because they're missing out on so much. Ignoring God is not the wisest thing to do. Others, perhaps, can see God's fingerprints in creation, but don't know who God is because they haven't been told about Him. This could be an opportunity for us to share our faith with others.

 ## *Challenge*

Are we ready to see God at work in the world around us? When we admire nature, let's remember the designer and give Him some praise.

CORE THEME | CREATION

Wise God

READ: ISAIAH 40:12–15

KEY VERSE V13
'Who can fathom the Spirit of the Lord, or instruct the Lord as his counsellor?'

Sometimes in life, things don't happen in the way we want or expect them to. Maybe you have met someone you really liked. You have shared similar interests and enjoyed being together. It seems as though the relationship might develop, when something happens that puts an end to any daydreams of a romantic future. It might be that he or she meets someone else, or that they have to move away for various reasons. Understandably, this can be painful and unsettling.

At times like these, it can be easy to grumble at God and sulk because He hasn't worked things out our way. Actually, when we do that, what we're saying to God is that we think we know better than He does. Isaiah shows us that thinking like this is just foolish. He does this by reminding us who God is and what He has done. Our God put the mountains together. His hands are big enough to hold the oceans. If God is this big and this powerful, what makes us think that we could know better than Him? Our God is incredibly creative and awesomely powerful, and He's also infinitely wise. Even if we don't understand what God is doing in a particular situation, His way is always the best.

 Pray
Are you or is someone you know going through a difficult situation? Spend some time praying about it. Then trust God to deal with the problem – He has got your best interests at heart.

CORE THEME | CREATION

Perfect future

 READ: ROMANS 8:18–25

KEY VERSES VV20–21
*'creation itself will be liberated from its bondage to
decay and brought into the freedom and glory of the
children of God.'*

You've probably noticed that, although the world is an
amazing place, there are times when things go wrong
with it. We've all seen images in the news of the scenes
after earthquakes, freak storms or volcanic eruptions. In
September 2017, hurricane Irma hit the Caribbean and
Florida causing catastrophic damage and fatalities. So
if creation is good, and the God who created it is good,
why do awful things like these happen? That's a difficult
question to answer, but these verses from Romans give us
a few clues.

The world is flawed – under a curse (v20) – not because
God planned it this way, but as a result of the Fall (see
Gen. 3:17–19). The devil loves to destroy anything good,
and we can see his influence in the world. We're all flawed
too (v23). All too often, it's our choices that damage
ourselves, the people around us, and creation as well.
However, in Romans 8, the apostle Paul tells us something
really important: whatever the reasons for the flaws in
creation, one day God will make it perfect! He'll make us
and the whole of creation new and flawless – and pain and
suffering will end.

 ## *Pray*
*Lord God, please break the devil's influence on the world.
Thank You that, one day, You'll make everything new and
flawless and exactly as You want it. Amen.*

DATING

A match made in heaven

READ: GENESIS 2:18–24

KEY VERSE V18
'The LORD God said, "It is not good for the man to be alone. I will make a helper suitable for him."'

Dating: what connotations does this word have for you? Are they positive or negative? Perhaps you're in a long-term committed relationship. Perhaps you enjoy playing the field. Or maybe you just wish you could find your soul mate. Do you think God has anything to say about dating? Over the next couple of weeks, we will begin to find out what the Bible has to tell us about this important area of life.

Dating is a relatively modern phenomenon, so there are not many explicit references to dating, as we would understand it, in the Bible. However, the Bible has a lot to say about relationships in general, and this can shed important light on what God might say to us about our dating habits today.

First and foremost, God created us to be people in relationship with others – relationships of all kinds. During creation, God would review what He had created that day and pronounce that it was good. In today's key verse, we read about the first time God found something in His creation that wasn't good: 'It is not good for the man to be alone' (Gen. 2:18). God recognised that Adam was lonely. God saw that Adam could be, and do, much more with a companion.

God's intention was that Adam and Eve would be created different but equal. Each helping and supporting the other in every area of life. In view of this, let's look at our closest relationships. Do the people closest to us support us in every area of our lives? In particular, do they help us to live the life that God intends for us and do the work that He is calling us to do?

Think

Whether you are currently dating or not, think about your closest relationships. Do your close friends support you in living your life for Christ, or do they hinder this?

Three – the magic number

READ: ECCLESIASTES 4:9–12

KEY VERSE V12
'Three are even better, for a triple-braided cord is not easily broken.' (NLT)

Today's reading reinforces that God's intention for us is to be in relationships with others. There are many advantages to supporting and being supported by very close friends. Look through today's passage – what advantages are listed to being in a pair? What other advantages could you add to these from your own experience?

Just like we saw yesterday, God sees our need for companionship. However, rather than just stopping at saying that two are better than one, this passage says that 'Three are even better' (v12, NLT).

This passage reminds us of a very important truth. No matter how good our earthly relationships might be, including God in them will strengthen and enhance them to their full potential. Yes – the third person is God.

The image of the cord is very powerful too. It suggests that God should not be an optional extra in our relationships. Rather, He should be entwined with us; deeply involved in our relationships and just as important as each of the people involved. By including God in your relationships, those relationships will become richer and stronger.

Pray

Invite God to become part of your earthly relationships. Ask Him to strengthen them and make them healthy and sustaining.

HOT TOPIC | DATING

It's not my fault

READ: GENESIS 3:11–13

KEY VERSE V12
'The man said, "The woman you put here with me – she gave me some fruit from the tree, and I ate it."'

We have already seen that God recognises mankind's need for relationships. We have seen how He provided Eve as a companion for Adam and that this relationship was part of His perfect plan for mankind. However, this relationship was not without its problems!

In today's reading, we return to the story of Adam and Eve after they have sinned by eating the fruit that God had forbidden them to eat. They both know that they have done wrong, and unsuccessfully try to hide from God. When God confronts them, they give excuses and try to avoid any blame.

One of the common pitfalls within relationships is doing something you know is wrong, and then trying to blame the other person. When we are close to other people, all too often we can find it easy to blame them for our own mistakes and wrongdoing. It is no use hiding from God, though – He can see what's in our hearts. And reflecting back on yesterday's passage, we need to be completely honest and open with Him, remembering that He is the third person in our relationships.

HOT TOPIC | DATING

➕ *Challenge*

How much do you take responsibility for your own actions and how often do you try to pass the blame on to others? Are there any bad habits within your relationships that you need to step up and change?

The right path

READ: PROVERBS 4:23–27

KEY VERSE V23
'Guard your heart above all else, for it determines the course of your life.' (NLT)

Spend a few minutes reflecting on this verse from Proverbs. How much do you think it's true for you that 'your heart... determines the course of your life' (Prov. 4:23, NLT)? If you think that you love someone, does this change the way you see your life and the path set out for your future?

Perhaps you feel that a particular university course would be good for you, but you are considering not going because you can't bear the thought of being away from your boyfriend/girlfriend. Perhaps you always thought you would want to take a gap year to serve God, but now you're having second thoughts because of how it might affect your relationship.

A strong and healthy relationship is a wonderful thing, but it should not stop us from following where God leads us – and after all, aren't we here to live out His will, not our own? Let's make it our number one priority to 'Seek the Kingdom of God above all else'. God knows us better than we know ourselves. If you can put your trust in Him and seek His will, you can be confident that He will 'give you everything you need' (Matt. 6:33). That includes the certainty of knowing that you are unconditionally loved by your heavenly Father.

Think

Today's passage talks about us making a straight path for our feet. How far do you let God guide you in your decisions, and how much are you influenced by your relationships?

HOT TOPIC | DATING

Help or hindrance

READ: ACTS 20:18–27

KEY VERSE V24
'I consider my life worth nothing to me; my only aim is to finish the race and complete the task the Lord Jesus has given me'

There are many dating sites and apps around the world for all age groups. A lot of people are searching for close, meaningful relationships. Fairytales and romantic films fuel the belief that being loved by other people is the real sign of having value and worth.

However, this view that you have to be in a romantic relationship to have any kind of value is not true. In the Bible, Paul tells us that our lives are made worthwhile by doing what God wants us to do and completing 'the task the Lord Jesus has given' (Acts 20:24). This is something we can do whether we are single or in a relationship.

In one of his letters, Paul highlights that we may be better able to focus on doing God's work when we are single. But perhaps the most important verse to reflect on is this: 'I want you to do whatever will help you serve the Lord best, with as few distractions as possible' (1 Cor. 7:35, NLT). Only you can know if your relationships are a hindrance or a help. The right person will be a support for you as you seek God together.

HOT TOPIC | DATING

✚ *Challenge*

God has a plan for you and for your life. Are any of your relationships hindering you in that? Do you need to let a relationship go so that you can serve God more faithfully?

Shared faith

READ: 2 CORINTHIANS 6:14–16

KEY VERSES VV14–15
'Don't team up with those who are unbelievers… How can a believer be a partner with an unbeliever?' (NLT)

Do you remember sports days at your primary school? You may have had to take part in a three-legged race. You and your partner are tied together at your ankles and you have to run as fast as possible to the finishing line. Both of you are trying to get into a rhythm and head in the same direction. However, it is not easy, particularly if you both have different ideas about how to go about it. Imagine what a disaster it would be if you wanted to go in different directions.

Whether or not we should date people who aren't Christians is a contentious issue. But these verses from 2 Corinthians highlight a problem with that kind of relationship. Whatever our relationship status, our ultimate focus should be in living out God's will for our lives. How can we do that if the person we're dating doesn't share that focus?

It's not that dating a non-Christian is 'wrong', but it isn't ideal. How can we form a lasting, supportive relationship with someone who we differ with on issues of belief? Where something as important as faith isn't shared between the two people, it's not fair for either person.

HOT TOPIC | DATING

Pray

Thank God for couples you know who have supported each other in their walk with God. Ask God to help Christians in relationships with non-Christians to keep their focus on Him.

Weekend

19/20 MAY

I just called to say...

READ: PSALM 37:23–26

KEY VERSE V23
'The Lord directs the steps of the godly. He delights in every detail of their lives'.' (NLT)

Have you ever spent ages on hold to a call centre somewhere? You ring them with an important question but end up waiting to talk to someone for what feels like forever, being told repeatedly by a recorded message that, 'Your call is important to us'. It would be easy to think that the call really can't be that important to them if they won't answer it!

When we talk to God, He is always there to listen to us. He has a limitless ability to hear everyone, all over the world, all the time. In one passage in the New Testament we read that God even knows each individual sparrow (Luke 12:6). The passage goes on to say that we are worth more than many sparrows. So God knows even more about us, including the number of hairs on our heads.

Of course, God is concerned with the big, important, global issues. But, today's reading tells us that God 'delights in every detail' of our lives. This includes our love life! He cares about how we are feeling, who we are falling for, and what worries us. He wants to be included in these details and wants us to share our hopes and fears with Him. Remember that God is interested in all aspects of your life and loves to hear from you.

Over the next week we will be looking at the love-lives of a few people in the Bible. In the same way that God cares about us, these people's relationships were important to Him. As we read their stories, reflect on how you think their relationships affected their ability to serve God and live out their God-given purposes.

➕ Challenge

Spend some time talking with God now about your private thoughts and what's really on your mind and heart. Remember that God 'delights in every detail' of your life. You can trust Him with anything.

Worth waiting for

READ: GENESIS 29:14–30

KEY VERSE V20
'So Jacob served seven years to get Rachel, but they seemed like only a few days to him because of his love for her.'

Have you ever tried to do anything to prove your love for someone? Perhaps you've bought an extravagant gift, or agreed to do some kind of horrible task for them. In today's reading, we see how Jacob has fallen for Rachel and agreed to work for her father for seven years. (Yes, really! That's the equivalent of school years 7–13!)

At the end of these seven years of labour, Jacob is tricked. Rather than being given Rachel as his wife, he is given her older sister, Leah. After Jacob's protests, he is given Rachel as his wife as well, but has to work an additional seven years for her! Now we're looking at the equivalent of years 7–13, three years of university and four years of work after that! Would you be prepared to work that long for anyone, no matter how much you loved them? What about just waiting that long? Perhaps you are waiting for that person now, either waiting to meet the right person or to be in a relationship with someone in particular.

God set us a great example of going to extreme lengths to show His love – He sent His only Son to die so that we could know Him. He was that desperate for a relationship with us.

HOT TOPIC | DATING

Think
When we are waiting for the one we love (or will love), how can we have the right patient attitude?

True love

READ: GENESIS 29:31–35

KEY VERSE V31
*'When the LORD saw that Leah was not loved, he
enabled her to conceive, but Rachel remained childless.'*

When we looked at yesterday's passage from Genesis, who
did you most identify with in the story? Perhaps it wasn't
so much Jacob, working for 14 years to win the woman he
loved. Perhaps you feel that you're more like Leah, the
misfit; the one who always seems to get left behind when
everyone else is dating. Even if you don't identify with Leah,
you can probably think of someone you know who fits that
description – an unconventional but wonderful person!

Thankfully, the story isn't all bad for Leah. In today's
reading, it continues and we see that God saw Leah's
suffering and blessed her by enabling her to give birth to
several children.

If you feel insignificant in the eyes of your peers, then
take heart from this story. God sees your pain and He loves
you dearly. We mentioned at the weekend that God is
concerned with every detail of our lives. Leah's story is a
real illustration of this.

By the way, notice that Leah always made an effort to
try to find love and acceptance from her husband. But
when she has her last son she says, 'This time I will praise
the LORD' (Gen. 29:35), finally acknowledging the true
source of love and acceptance.

Pray
*Father God, we all feel unlovable sometimes. Help me to
remember and find lasting comfort in the love that You
have for me. Amen.*

HOT TOPIC | DATING

'That girl was no good for me'

READ: JUDGES 16:4–21

KEY VERSE V15
'[Delilah] said to him, "How can you say, 'I love you,' when you won't confide in me?"'

Have you ever heard the phrase 'love is blind'? Perhaps the story of Samson and Delilah illustrates that idea. Samson falls in love with Delilah, but seems oblivious to the fact that Delilah clearly doesn't feel the same way. Delilah sees her relationship with Samson as an opportunity to make money. All she needs to do is get Samson to tell her the secret of his strength. Initially Samson tells her lies, which she acts on to try to bring about his downfall. In the light of this, Samson, very foolishly and after constant nagging and blackmail from Delilah, gives in and tells her everything. But, as we have said, love can be blind.

Sometimes our love for someone can make us do things we later regret. We can be persuaded to do unwise things by someone we think we love. This might mean going further in our physical relationship than we want to, spending all our money on extravagant gifts, or making unwise decisions about our future to impress them. When we want to please someone we care about, it can be very difficult to say no.

HOT TOPIC | DATING

Think

Can you think of any situations where you are under pressure to do something you don't think is right? What can we learn from the story of Samson and Delilah?

Should I stay or should I go?

READ: MATTHEW 1:18–25

KEY VERSE V24
*'When Joseph woke up, he did what the angel of the
Lord had commanded and took Mary home as his wife.'*

Joseph and Mary are one of the most inspiring couples in
the Bible. We're going to spend the next two days looking
at their story and what we can learn from them.

Imagine what Joseph goes through. He is meant to be
marrying Mary but then finds out she is pregnant. He
knows that the baby is not his, and therefore he feels
the only real option for him is to end their relationship.
Imagine how you would feel if you were in his situation.
Most people would do the same and decide to end the
relationship on the quiet. But then, when an angel appears
to Joseph and tells him to take Mary as his wife, Joseph
obeys God's command. However hard it must have
seemed, Joseph acted honourably and with dignity.

Sometimes our relationships hit tricky patches and
we're not sure whether we're doing the right thing in
staying with that person. But as we've already said, God
cares about all the details of our lives and He wants to
guide us. Are we open to His guidance on whether or not
we should stay in a relationship with somebody?

 Pray

*Father God, thank You for Joseph's example in following
Your guidance even when it was hard. Please help me to be
as ready as Joseph to obey You in relationships, even when
this doesn't seem like the logical thing to do. Amen.*

HOT TOPIC | DATING

Love on the run

READ: MATTHEW 2:13–23

KEY VERSE V13
'escape to Egypt. Stay there until I tell you, for Herod is going to search for the child to kill him.'

Yesterday we took a look at Joseph's willingness to obey God in his relationship with Mary. However, the difficult times were far from over after Jesus was born, as Herod shows in today's reading just how far he is prepared to go to make sure there's no other king to threaten him. In order to avoid the massacre of infants, Joseph and Mary take the young Jesus and escape to Egypt. Finally, quite some time later, God commands them to go back to Israel.

All the accounts regarding Joseph and Mary in the Bible reveal that they were always obedient to God's commands. They stick together, even when life is scary, confusing and uncertain, and support each other in trying to live as God wants them to. What a great example for us as we seek to form our own God-honouring relationships.

Life isn't always rosy, but God calls us to support and encourage each other in the hard times, whether in romantic relationships or as friends and families. We have already looked at the fact that God recognises our need for relationship. He doesn't want us to be alone but wants us to have people who can support us in living out His will for us – just as Joseph and Mary supported each other.

HOT TOPIC | DATING

➕ *Challenge*
When life gets hard, how does it affect your relationships? Are you committed to the people closest to you? Or do you lash out and shut yourself off from them?

**WEEKEND
26/27 MAY**

MONEY

Money, money, money

READ: MATTHEW 6:19–34

KEY VERSE V21
*'For where your treasure is, there your
heart will be also.'*

Over the next couple of weeks we're going to be
thinking about money, and what our attitude as
Christians should be towards it. Money is something
that can occupy a lot of a person's thinking space – if
they feel they don't have enough, they worry about
getting more – and if they feel they have a lot, they
worry about keeping it safe.

Interestingly, Jesus talks quite a lot about money
and He tells a number of stories that involve it,
particularly as recorded in Luke's Gospel in chapters
18–22. Jesus never says that we should keep away
from money – He recognises that it's part of our daily

life and a key means of survival. However, He does warn us about the hold that money can have over us, if we treat it as more important than it really is. Jesus tells stories of what happens when money becomes our security, or when it becomes a way in which we measure our status.

In today's reading, Jesus warns about what happens when money becomes our focus. If it becomes our 'treasure', then that's what we will value and concentrate on, rather than trusting God. He makes it very clear that we cannot focus on both God and money – when we look at one, we will turn our backs on the other. We shouldn't get caught up in the money obsession that the world has, because God will provide us with all that we need. If we believe that to be true, then we will be able to be generous with what we have, whether that's a lot or just a little.

Think

As you read through this passage, which of the things that Jesus mentions do you find yourself worrying most about? Clothes? Food? Where you live? How do you respond to what Jesus says about worrying about those things?

I want it all

READ: LUKE 12:13–34

KEY VERSE V15
'Beware! Guard against every kind of greed. Life is not measured by how much you own.' (NLT)

Many adverts on television are aimed at encouraging you to buy a new car, a new phone, new perfume or aftershave. The advertising industry spends millions ensuring their adverts are sleek and send exactly the right message to the viewers. So often these days, that message is that you are what you own, so it had better be the best and the latest if you want people to think well of you. The advertising business depends on us always being dissatisfied with what we currently have, and always wanting more and better.

Jesus' response to someone who wanted more was to tell a story. He told a parable about a man who lived his life in pursuit of more, who thought that his worth was measured by the volume of what he owned, and that the security of his future depended upon it. Sadly, the man in the story found out the hard way that he had put his security in the wrong things. All his gains turned out to be for nothing.

It's very easy for us to fall into this trap too. So, we need to guard ourselves against this way of thinking and find our worth and security in our relationship with God and all He has blessed us with.

Challenge
The next time you see an advert and you're tempted to buy the product in question, ask yourself what your real reason is for wanting it. Is it really something you need?

Money trap

READ: LUKE 18:18–30

KEY VERSE V22
'Sell everything you have and give to the poor, and you will have treasure in heaven. Then come, follow me.'

This has got to be one of the saddest stories recorded in the Gospels. It's the story of a rich young man who desperately wanted to be right with God, but wasn't willing to make God the priority in his life. In many other areas he had been able to act in the right way, but when it came to parting with his money, he just couldn't do it. Jesus knew that as long as these things were so important to him, the man wouldn't truly be able to follow Him.

Jesus isn't saying that it's wrong to be rich. But He is saying that it is damaging when money has such a strong hold on us that we can't bear to give it away. The rich young man thought that what he wanted more than anything was eternal life, but Jesus exposed what was really going on in his heart – the man did want treasure in heaven, but he also wanted to hold on to his treasure on earth.

Jesus' promise to everyone listening was that if you are willing to give up what you have for His sake, you won't regret it: you will have what you need in this life and gain the eternal life that the young man so desperately wanted.

HOT TOPIC | MONEY

Pray

God, help me to look honestly at my priorities to see if there is anything that I place more importance on than You. Please help me to put You first. Amen.

Change of heart

 READ: LUKE 19:1-10

KEY VERSE V9
'Today salvation has come to this house, because this man, too, is a son of Abraham.'

In the passage we looked at yesterday from Luke 18, Jesus says that it's hard for the rich to enter the kingdom of God, but that all things are possible with God – even changing a person's heart. Here, we have the evidence of that. It's the story of a rich man – and not just rich, but deceitful too – whose heart was changed completely when he met Jesus.

Tax collectors were notorious in Israel for not just collecting taxes that were owed, but for collecting more than was necessary and keeping it for themselves. Zacchaeus was a chief tax collector and had become very wealthy from his ill-gotten gains. The bystanders were extremely disgruntled that Jesus would have tea with a man like this, but Jesus knew exactly what Zacchaeus was like and the place that money had in his life. Zacchaeus realised that he couldn't be a friend of Jesus and continue with his life as it was, so he immediately committed to paying back much more than he'd taken and giving half of his wealth to the poor. In doing these things, he proved that money was no longer his priority; Jesus was.

 ## *Think*

Jesus said that Zacchaeus became a son of Abraham; someone who, like Abraham, believed in God and proved that by what he did. Does the way you handle money demonstrate what you believe?

HOT TOPIC | MONEY

Two copper coins

READ: LUKE 21:1–4

KEY VERSE V4
'All these people gave their gifts out of their wealth; but she out of her poverty put in all she had to live on.'

For the disciples, life with Jesus must have meant being constantly challenged on what they thought they knew. You can just imagine them standing with Jesus and watching the crowds making their offerings in the Temple, being really impressed with the amounts of money that some people put in the collection box. In the eyes of the disciples, these people were incredibly generous. But this turns out to be another of those challenging moments for the disciples as Jesus gives them a powerful lesson on giving. He would have known that the disciples respected those who gave the most, but the person who caught Jesus' attention was the poor widow who gave just a couple of pennies.

For Jesus, generosity is not defined by how much you give; it's about how much of a sacrifice it is for you to give. Jesus wanted the disciples to know that although they might be impressed by large offerings, those rich people would barely feel the impact of what they'd given. On the other hand, the widow would feel it deeply and immediately. She was the one who gave until it hurt and trusted God to provide for what she herself needed. She was the one who was truly generous.

HOT TOPIC | MONEY

Pray

Thank You, Jesus, that You are not impressed by the amount of money that we give, but the heart with which we give it. Please help me to be truly generous. Amen.

Declutter and depend on God

READ: HEBREWS 13:1–6

KEY VERSE V5
*'be content with what you have, because God has said,
"Never will I leave you; never will I forsake you."'*

There is a book by Jen Hatmaker called 7.* It is a record of a project that Jen undertook when she became shocked at her level of consumerism. Jen realised that she wasn't simply buying stuff (as we all do); she was buying stuff in ever-greater amounts and was never really satisfied with what she had.

So, Jen decided to tackle her excesses in clothing, shopping, waste, food, possessions, media and stress. She set herself the challenge of living with just seven things in each of these areas. For one month, she only allowed herself to wear seven items of clothing (not including underwear!). Through it, she was appalled at how many clothes she owned but never wore. But what upset her more was how much she relied on her clothes to give her identity and how much she worried about what others would think of her. She was depending on these things to give her what only God could.

Consumerism always leaves us wanting more. It will never really satisfy us. God longs for us to be satisfied in Him alone, to look to Him for our identity and to know that we can depend on Him to be with us always.

Challenge

How much of a consumer do you think you are? How much of what you own do you actually use? If you own stuff you never use, give it away.

*Jen Hatmaker, 7 (Nashville, TN. USA: Broadman & Holman, 2012)

Weekend

2/3 JUN

Rich in generosity

READ: 1 TIMOTHY 6:6–10

KEY VERSE V10
'For the love of money is a root of all kinds of evil. Some people, eager for money, have wandered from the faith'

This has got to be one of the most often misquoted verses in the Bible! You may well have heard people quote that 'money is the root of all evil', but that's not what Paul says. It's the *love of money* that causes trouble, and in the situation that Paul is writing to Timothy about, it's causing people to neglect their faith and prioritise the pursuit of wealth. Money has become their god.

There is nothing wrong with money and possessions in themselves, which you may be relieved to hear as you look around your room at your possessions! The problems come, as we have seen over this last week, from the position they occupy in our lives and our attitude towards them. When they become our god, we are in real danger.

As you read about the first Christians in the New Testament, you see that they didn't make a priority of material riches: far from it. They very often gave money away and shared possessions. They strove to become rich in faith, rich in generosity and rich in good deeds. These are the riches that we should love. Paul tells Timothy to urge the people around him who are materially rich to aim for riches in other ways instead.

In Philippians (also written by Paul), he says that he has learned to be content whatever the circumstances. He has known times when he had plenty, and has known times when he had very little, yet in all those times he knew real contentment because he knew God. He'd enjoyed things when he had them but he didn't sink into despair when he didn't.

Challenge

If you're able to, make a point this week of giving away more money than you usually would. For example, why not start a regular monthly donation to a charity, or give one larger gift to your church for something specific?

Good stewards

READ: 1 TIMOTHY 6:17-21

KEY VERSE V18
*'Command them to do good, to be rich in good deeds,
and to be generous and willing to share.'*

Cambodia is one of the poorest countries in the world.
There is widespread poverty, high unemployment,
inadequate hygiene conditions that have led to diseases.
Over 10% of children die before reaching the age of five
and life expectancy is around 50 years old. Many people
have little more than the clothes they are wearing.
The reality is that, if you are born in the West, you are
extremely privileged and rich compared with people in
Cambodia, even if you don't think you are.

Perhaps we can start to feel guilty about this disparity
of wealth, and maybe even consider giving away all our
possessions. But trying to live like Cambodians isn't the
answer. Instead, we should let our knowledge of how little
some people have prompt us to be good stewards of all
that we have. Most of us have been blessed with a nice
home and a little bit of money, but they are gifts from God
that we can use to be a blessing to other people. When we
have the attitude that everything we have is a gift from
God, it changes our hearts and loosens our grip on our
money and possessions. God has entrusted us with good
things and wants us to be generous with them.

HOT TOPIC | MONEY

Think

*Do you see all that you have been given as a gift from
God? How would it change the way in which you treat your
possessions if you believed that? Are you a good steward?*

Three jars

READ: PHILIPPIANS 4:10–20

KEY VERSE V19
'And my God will meet all your needs according to the riches of his glory in Christ Jesus.'

Yesterday's notes were about being a good steward of our money and possessions. But how do we go about doing that practically? If you are struggling with how to manage your money, one idea is to have three jars labelled: 'Spend', 'Save' and 'Give'. Whenever you get some money, whether pocket money, birthday money or money earned, you can distribute it amongst the three jars. If there's something you would really like, wait until there is enough money in the 'Spend' jar before buying it. This means that you are able to get the nice things that you like, but often not immediately, and not at the expense of being able to respond to other people's needs. You could maybe continue this practice with bank accounts rather than jars!

The Bible doesn't say that it's wrong to have nice things. In fact there are many stories of rich people who were followers of God in the Bible, such as Lydia who traded in purple cloth and Cornelius the centurion who was very generous to the poor. The key thing is that these things don't consume us, and that we are still able to be generous to others.

HOT TOPIC | MONEY

Challenge

Why not try the 'three jar' model suggested today? Ask God to guide you in your saving, spending and giving.

Giving joyfully

READ: DEUTERONOMY 14:22–29

KEY VERSE V22
*'Be sure to set aside a tenth of all that your fields
produce each year.'*

The idea of giving is not a new one for Christians; God has
instilled it in His people from long ago. In this reading
we see God instructing the Israelites to give 10% of what
they harvest back to Him. This has continued to be a rule
of thumb amongst Christians. If you hear people talking
about tithing, this is what it means.

The reality is, though, that this was just the beginning!
On top of the tithe, the people were instructed to leave
some crops in their fields for the poor to harvest and to
give money to the priests, and to give further gifts for
festivals and sacrifices. They really ended up giving more
like 25% of their income.

In the New Testament, the theme of giving is still very
present, but it talks in terms of people giving cheerfully
and generously, rather than a specific amount. The key
thing in both the Old and New Testaments is that giving is
meant to be something to be celebrated. It's a joyful thing,
because it recognises that God has given us good things
and reminds us to thank Him for that. So the question isn't,
'How little can I get away with giving?' but, 'How generous
and cheerful can I be in what I give?'

HOT TOPIC | MONEY

Pray
*Lord, sometimes it feels hard to think about giving away
what I have, especially if I don't think I have very much.
Please help me to know real joy in being generous. Amen.*

All good gifts around us

READ: DEUTERONOMY 8:6–18

KEY VERSE V18
'But remember the LORD your God, for it is he who gives you the ability to produce wealth'

With all this talk of giving you may still be wondering why you should. After all, aren't your money and possessions yours to do what you like with? Especially if you worked hard to earn the money to buy them in the first place.

This is precisely the situation that God was addressing with the Israelites. He had brought them through the wilderness into the land that He had promised, flowing with milk and honey – meaning it was a rich and fertile land. They would be able to eat well, enjoy good harvests and prosper because resources were readily available. God knew that very quickly they would become rich and comfortable, so He warns them not to become proud in their wealth and plush homes. He wants them to remember the story of where they came from; how it was He who brought them to this beautiful place and gave them skills to enable them to earn their living.

When we are tempted to think that we have done everything on our own, we too should remember that warning. Let's stop and thank God for giving us the ability to thrive and the skills we use to earn our living.

Think

How would you respond to someone who says they have no need to thank God or give money away, because they are 'self-made'?

HOT TOPIC | MONEY

Heavenly provision

 READ: PSALM 34:1–10

KEY VERSE: V8
'Taste and see that the LORD is good; blessed is the one who takes refuge in him.'

In 1836, George Müller and his wife opened their home to 30 orphans. Over the years this number grew so much that they had to build five homes to accommodate all the children. Despite the huge costs of building and running these homes, Müller never asked people for money to support this work. He told many stories of how they received donations of food just when they were needed, to feed the children. One breakfast time, when there was no food in the house, Müller got the children to sit down at the breakfast table and give thanks for their food. Just as they finished praying, there was a knock on the door and the baker stood there with enough bread to feed everyone. And just a moment later, the milkman's cart broke down right in front of their house, so he asked if they would like the milk as he could no longer deliver it!

Time and time again God tells us not to worry about our situation. He knows what we need and has promised to provide for us if we trust in Him. He doesn't want us to become so preoccupied with money and possessions that we forget to trust Him. If we don't trust Him, we don't have the joy of seeing Him keep His promises to us.

HOT TOPIC | MONEY

 Pray
Thank You, Lord, that You are good. Please help me to trust You in all situations. I trust Your promise that I will never lack anything I need. Amen.

01

**WEEKEND
9/10 JUN**

APOLOGETICS

The good book

READ: 2 TIMOTHY 3:10–17

KEY VERSE V16
'All Scripture is God-breathed and is useful for teaching, rebuking, correcting and training in righteousness'

Welcome back to the Apologetics series. If you read through the January–April *Mettle*, you'll have covered a whole load of important apologetics-related material already. But don't worry if you missed it – there's some great stuff to come, with plenty to discuss, think and pray about.

The last issue looked at the importance of being able to explain what we believe and why. Some of the common arguments atheists raise against the Christian faith, and how we can counter those arguments, were explored. They included the accusations that God is a bully, doesn't make any difference in the world and doesn't exist anyway. In this issue of *Mettle*, we're picking up where we left off last time: unpacking more important truths about our God and our world. Keep in mind that Apologetics doesn't mean 'apologising' for what we believe, but explaining it and supporting our views. It's about building bridges with people who believe different things, not about getting defensive.

Let's kick off by asking a few questions about the Bible. How do we know the Bible is reliable? Is it really relevant to us? And what are we supposed to make of those weird bits in Leviticus? A good place to start is the truth that the Bible is inspired by God. God speaks to us through it; guiding us, challenging us and helping us to live His way. The Bible is a helpful user manual for living a godly life. The real question is not whether the Bible is important and relevant, but how we interpret it in a way that is faithful to the person of Jesus – the focus of the whole book.

Think

How can we understand what God wants to say to us through a passage from the Bible? Is it enough to just read the words on the page?

Signpost to God

READ: HEBREWS 4:12–16

KEY VERSE V12
'For the word of God is alive and active. Sharper than any double-edged sword, it penetrates even to dividing soul and spirit... it judges the thoughts and attitudes'

'A good Samaritan.' 'A mass Exodus.' 'A Judas.' 'No rest for the wicked.' There is something about the words of the Bible that lodges in our minds and hearts, as individuals and as a society. There's something about the Bible that registers with us, no matter which culture or era we read it in.

The Bible is hugely relevant to us – uncomfortably so at times. God has a way of speaking through the Bible to challenge us on very specific things in our lives. It's true that the newest parts of the Bible were written nearly 2,000 years ago, but the truths and principles within the pages speak to people's hearts just as directly now as when the words were first written. It's almost as if the book itself is alive as God breathes His life into it, making it powerful, inspiring, challenging and uplifting.

But just to clarify: the Bible contains enormous power, but it gains its power from God. So the Bible is not the end in itself, but something that points us towards God, and inspires us to worship Him. The Bible is the means by which we understand the God we worship and let Him guide us.

Pray
Thank God for the ways in which He speaks to us and inspires us through the Bible. Ask that He will use it to reveal more of Himself to you.

HOT TOPIC | APOLOGETICS

Holy Ghost writers

 READ: 2 PETER 1:12–21

KEY VERSES VV20–21
*'Above all, you must understand that no prophecy of
Scripture came about by the prophet's own interpretation
of things... but prophets... spoke from God'*

So how does that work? How can the Bible have been
simultaneously written by God and people? Some people
find this idea confusing. Others write it off as nonsense,
without even really thinking about it. Was God leaning
over the writers' shoulders as they put pen to papyrus? Or
were these guys just puppets, with God controlling their
writing hands?

However it happened, God prompted each of the
Bible's forty or so writers to record what they had seen,
heard and experienced of life. But also God's words and
actions. God let each of these writers use their own skill,
perspectives and personalities to do that, but inspired
them as they wrote. In this way, although the Bible was
written by human beings (and only a fraction of it contains
words explicitly spoken by God), God communicates His
truth through these words.

It's very unlikely that God dictated where every last
comma of the Bible should go, but we can wholeheartedly
believe that God can and does speak to us through all of
it. So the Bible carries real authority. Let's read it with
respect and admiration for the God who inspires it.

 Challenge
*Do you take the Bible seriously? As you read it, remember who
inspires it and expect God to challenge you and guide you.*

HOT TOPIC | APOLOGETICS

Nitty gritty

≡ **READ: LEVITICUS 19:11–22**

KEY VERSE V19

'*Do not mate different kinds of animals. Do not plant your field with two kinds of seed. Do not wear clothing woven of two kinds of material.*'

What are your trainers made out of? Most trainers are made from a combination of leather, synthetic rubber and fabric. Does that mean we disobey God by wearing them? Is anybody who wears leather elbow patches on their tweed jacket in danger of the fires of hell? Well, obviously not. But this is an example of a verse that people sometimes use to argue that the Bible is irrelevant. If we ignore this commandment, why should we take any notice of other commandments or teaching?

Some of the Bible's teachings are rooted in the time and culture in which they were written. (For example, Leviticus was written for a nation who spent 40 years in the desert. In that environment, poor quality clothing would have fallen apart.) But the majority of the Bible has plenty of things to teach us, for today in our everyday lives and situations. Even the random stuff about different kinds of cloth tells us that God can be gloriously practical in His guidance. He cares about every single area of our lives. This is good news, but also a challenge. If God really cares about everything we do, there's no area of our lives where compromising, or ignoring Him, is OK.

HOT TOPIC | APOLOGETICS

Think

Context is very important when reading the Bible, but some things are very clear indeed. Is there any teaching in the Bible that you prefer to explain away, rather than obey?

How old?

READ: GENESIS 1:1–31

KEY VERSE V3
'And God said, "Let there be light," and there was light.'

Did God really create the world in six actual 24-hour days? This line of thought leaves us with a world that's approximately 6,000 years old, hence a 'Young Earth'. However, geological evidence and fossil records put the age of the earth at around 4.5 billion years. How do we explain the difference between the two figures?

Many people today believe that this passage was not meant to be taken literally, that instead it takes the form of an epic poem. This idea suggests that the 'six days' is poetic language, representing 'six ages' or 'six periods of time', which could explain the difference between the figures. On the other hand, many believe that it should be taken literally, and that we shouldn't try to fit God's work into our limited understanding – there are many things of God that we cannot comprehend as humans.

What we do know is that Genesis conveys that God is the almighty creator – that He, not any pagan god or random explosion is to be credited with creating the universe. We should take this truth absolutely seriously. The question, 'When was the world created?' is interesting to explore but even more important is the 'Who?' and 'Why?'

HOT TOPIC | APOLOGETICS

➕ Challenge
The timescale of creation and the age of the earth are complex issues. Look into this debate further, exploring both points of view.

Forbidden fruit

READ: GENESIS 3:1–19

KEY VERSE VV6–7
'So she took some of the fruit and ate it. Then she gave some to her husband... At that moment their eyes were opened, and they suddenly felt shame at their nakedness.' (NLT)

Do you enjoy eating sweets and chocolates? They are very tempting when displayed in shops, especially at Easter and Christmas. We know that they contain a lot of sugar and they are not very good for us, but we eat them anyway. In fact, in Britain we eat an average of 11kg of chocolate per person per year; that equates to about three bars a week.

Inside each of us there is a natural tendency to be drawn to forbidden things – things that harm ourselves and others. We have a natural tendency towards doing wrong things or, as the Bible says, sin. And our sin makes us ashamed, alienates us from God and damages our relationships with each other.

The time when Adam and Eve were evicted from the Garden of Eden is known as 'the Fall'. It describes the transition from innocent obedience to God to a state of guilty disobedience. Some people ask whether we can take this story literally. And as with the creation account, it's debatable whether it's historical or figurative. There are many debates out there, with good arguments for each side. But debates aside, let's take seriously the truth that it highlights: we are all flawed, foolish, self-destructive people, in dire need of a Saviour.

Think

What does the story of Adam and Eve say to you about human nature? What does it tell you about God?

HOT TOPIC | APOLOGETICS

Weekend

16/17 JUN

Old man Methuselah

READ: GENESIS 5:1–27

KEY VERSE V27
'Methuselah lived a total of 969 years,
and then he died.'

The longest living person since modern
records began was a French woman who died
in 1997 at the age of 122 years and 164 days.
Life expectancy does seem to be increasing
these days, largely thanks to better diet and
healthcare, but people still generally count
themselves lucky if they live into their 80s.
So with that kind of background, the idea of
someone living for nearly 1,000 years seems
more than a little far-fetched. Methuselah
and others in this chapter provide more
ammunition for people who label the Bible as
'unbelievable'.

So how do we explain Methuselah and his 969 years of life? Perhaps this chapter is based on a different understanding of periods of time, with a 'year' actually representing something far shorter. Or maybe, since this is a genealogy, the name of each man is a representation of the lifespan of his whole family. Neither of these theories holds much water though. Experts don't really give much credence to either. As crazy as it might sound, the most likely explanation is that Methuselah truly did live for 969 years! It is worth noting that many civilisations have records of surprisingly long lives in the distant past. So just maybe, we can take this passage from Genesis at face value.

In any case, in the next chapter, God limits people's lifespan to 120 years (see Genesis 6:3), which is almost exactly the same as the longest life on record. And if someone's greatest objection to believing the Bible is Methuselah's unusually long life, that's hardly a strong argument against the whole book!

 Pray

Ask for God's help in understanding the parts of the Bible that seem a little strange to you.

Stranger than fiction

 READ: JOSHUA 10:1–15

KEY VERSE V13
'So the sun stood still, and the moon stopped, till the nation avenged itself on its enemies'

So God made the sun stand still... Surely that didn't really happen. Things get exaggerated all the time in the stories of ancient heroes. Surely that's what's happened here in this episode from the life of Joshua. More than likely, it just felt as if the day was lasting longer than usual because of the intensity of the battle. We can't seriously be expected to believe this story, can we?

But hang on a minute. Even if this story is exaggerated, that doesn't mean it's not at least based on truth. And let's not forget that God is the one who created the sun in the first place. If we accept that, we must accept that He's capable of making the sun stand still, if He wants to. Just because it's extraordinary doesn't mean it's impossible.

There's an important principle at stake here. If we dismiss out of hand everything in the Bible that is outside of our normal experience, we remove its distinctiveness. The Bible is the story of salvation – God's power breaking into human experience to give us hope, security and peace. If we assume that miracles cannot be part of that story, we're robbing God of His power and reducing the Bible to a collection of meaningless fables.

 Challenge
Are there any parts of the Bible that you find difficult to believe? Why is that? Do you need to think again about any of this?

HOT TOPIC | APOLOGETICS

Different perspectives

READ: LUKE 23:26–43

KEY VERSE VV32–33
'Two other men, both criminals, were also led out with him to be executed... one on his right, the other on his left.'

There are people who think the Bible is full of contradictions. It's true that there are some passages that appear to have inconsistencies. But 'contradictions'?

Today's reading is an example of one of those inconsistencies. Luke mentions two criminals who are crucified alongside Jesus; one of them insulted Jesus, the other responded entirely and was saved as he died. Matthew's and Mark's versions of the same events say that both criminals insulted Jesus. John doesn't mention the criminals at all. Does that mean that all four writers are contradicting each other?

Imagine that you and three friends went to a party. A few days later, someone asks each of you to write down your version of what happened. Of course, all of you would write slightly different versions of events. You might put things in a slightly different order. One or two of you might mention things that the others had forgotten about or just didn't think were worth mentioning. Put together, your accounts would build up a rounded picture of what really happened at the party. In a similar way, we can argue that the four Gospels do not contradict each other. Rather, they work together to build a fuller picture of Jesus' life, death and resurrection.

HOT TOPIC | APOLOGETICS

Think

How would you respond to someone who claimed the Bible is full of contradictions?

To speak or not to speak

READ: PROVERBS 26:1–12

KEY VERSE VV4–5
*'Do not answer a fool according to his folly, or you
yourself will be just like him. Answer a fool according
to his folly, or he will be wise in his own eyes.'*

More today on the 'Is the Bible full of contradictions?'
issue. And actually, verses 4–5 do contradict each other.
There are reasons for that contradiction. The Proverbs are
short, punchy, memorable phrases which comment on the
realities of life, faith and relationships. They also highlight
that life is complex and unpredictable. For example, we
can respond to inaccurate and foolish statements about
faith and the Bible differently, according to the situation.
Sometimes it may be better not to waste time giving an
answer, or on other occasions a response might be of
benefit. This is where wisdom is needed. Yes, the writer
who wrote these verses is contradicting himself, but it's for
a purpose. It draws our attention to life's complexity.

There are passages from the Bible that we need to hold
in tension with others. For example, we must grapple with
the implications of the Old Testament teaching, 'an eye
for an eye' (Lev. 24:19–20) and Jesus urging us to turn the
other cheek (Matt. 5:39). But the contradictions in Proverbs
don't undermine the Bible. In fact, they make it more
down-to-earth and authentic.

HOT TOPIC | APOLOGETICS

Pray

*Lord God, thank You for understanding how complex and
unpredictable life can be. Thank You for being with us in
that complexity and helping us when we're confused. Amen.*

All creatures, great and small

READ: JOB 40:15–24

KEY VERSE V15
'Take a look at Behemoth, which I made, just as I made you.'

A new species of dinosaur was discovered in America in 2006, in the desert of Utah. Nasutoceratops is a member of the triceratops family, but has a huge nose and unusually long horns. Experts say it is unlike anything they have seen before. Dinosaurs are fascinating creatures and there's a lot of evidence for their existence. So how come the Bible doesn't mention them?

Well, there's a difference between the Bible not mentioning dinosaurs and it actively arguing that they never existed. The Bible isn't like a science textbook. It doesn't set out to describe every species that ever existed and exactly how they came into being. It focuses on the why of the whole thing: God as their creator. And on the other hand, maybe the Bible does mention dinosaurs after all. The description of 'Behemoth' in Job chapter 40 is uncannily similar to a large dinosaur. And in a similar way, Leviathan (mentioned in the next chapter and in Psalm 74) could be a plesiosaur – a prehistoric aquatic reptile. God made a huge variety of animals – there are currently 1,250,000 identified animal species. Maybe in Job's time there were more.

➕ Challenge

Do a bit of research into prehistoric life. It's fascinating stuff! If you've got a friend who knows a bit about this, pick their brain.

Dear God...

READ: PSALM 55:16–19

KEY VERSE V17
'Evening, morning and noon I cry out in distress, and he hears my voice.'

In the last couple of weeks, we've covered a lot of ground on the Bible. We've looked at whether it's reliable, believable and authoritative and how we respond to some of its apparent contradictions. Let's move on now and think about prayer. Sceptics often ask how we know that prayer makes any kind of difference. What makes us think that praying is anything more than words spoken into the air? Studies of hospital patients suggest that those who are prayed for recover more quickly and more fully than those who are not. But a cynic may argue that this is due to the power of positive thinking.

The most powerful evidence that God hears our prayers is our own, and others', experiences of prayers being answered. Some churches have a time during the service when people can share any answers to prayer. It could be recovery from illness, help with a difficult situation or even simply finding a lost item! These times of sharing God at work in the everyday are incredibly encouraging.

We might feel like our prayers are bouncing off the ceiling at times, but God truly is with us and listening when we pray. We might only see God's involvement in a situation in hindsight, but He is there, even if it doesn't feel like it.

HOT TOPIC | APOLOGETICS

Pray
Thank God for always being with you. Ask Him to help you to keep trusting Him, even when life gets tough.

**WEEKEND
23/24 JUNE**

CREATION

Messy lives

READ: GENESIS 3:1–19

KEY VERSE V17
'Cursed is the ground because of you'

For the majority of houses around the country, rubbish and recycling materials are collected once a week. Can you imagine if that did not happen? An average household throws away a tonne of waste every year and so very quickly our homes and streets would be filled with bags and bags of decomposing food, paper and packaging. This did happen for a time during the 'winter of discontent' of 1978–1979. During this very cold winter, there was a trade union general strike, which included the bin men. Rubbish was not collected, which caused rat infestations and foul smelling streets. That was 40 years ago and we produce a lot more rubbish and plastic these days. We are also more aware of the benefits of recycling, yet over half of our household waste is not recycled. There is a lot more that could be done in this area to improve this statistic. Glass, paper and cardboard are all materials that could be recycled.

God's plan is for us to take care of His creation, but how often do we not think about it? Small, careless actions like littering or not considering our carbon footprint can pollute the world and leave it in a real mess.

Today's reading in Genesis goes further than this too. In a way, every time we disobey God it has an impact on the world around us. When we go against God's plan, it damages us, it pollutes our relationships with other people, and it even pollutes God's creation. But when we obey God, our hearts and relationships are healed.

Think

Do any of your actions, however small, pollute the world around you? Do you disobey God by any of your actions? Say sorry to God for these things, and think of some ways in which you can help to clear up the mess in our world.

Heavenly doctor

READ: JOHN 3:16–21

KEY VERSE V17
'For God did not send his Son into the world to condemn the world, but to save the world through him.'

When we are feeling really ill, a visit to the doctor may be required. We make an appointment at the surgery, explain our symptoms to the doctor and wait for an expert diagnosis. How do doctors usually respond? Do they shout and yell at us because we are sick? Do they tell us what a terrible person we are for getting into that state? Of course not! That's not what doctors do. They take a good look at us, work out what the problem is and tell us what we need to do to get better. If we are sensible, we follow their advice.

Our world is 'sick'. People act and speak in ways that are selfish, irresponsible and hurtful. We see it all around us and, if we're honest, we know that we've acted like that ourselves. This behaviour leaves the world in a mess. But God had a plan. He sent Jesus into the world, not to shout and yell at everybody and tell us how terrible we are, but to show us the way to be healed.

Our sins and mistakes impact both us and our world, leaving it in a real mess. However, Jesus came to save us, forgive us and sort out the mess. God has a plan to save our world.

Pray

Lord Jesus, thank You for coming to forgive our sins and save the world. Thank You that I can be forgiven too. Please forgive me for all the times I've said and done things that were selfish and made the world more of a mess. Amen.

CORE THEME | CREATION 2

Choose life

READ: EPHESIANS 2:1–10

KEY VERSE V8

*'For it is by grace you have been saved, through faith…
it is the gift of God.'*

We mentioned yesterday that Jesus came into the world to save us and deal with our sin. This was God's plan to deal with the mess we'd made. Today, we find out that His plan is for everyone to be free from sin and to discover the amazing life He offers. It's a free gift! We can't do anything to deserve it, and all we need to do to receive it is to ask. But God doesn't force His plan on us – it's up to us individually to choose to accept it.

Yesterday, we thought about the times when we are sick and need to go to a doctor. The doctor helps us, and usually after that we are fine. But what if we decided we'd be OK and chose not to go to the doctor? If we'd been ill with something serious, it would have got worse and worse until maybe it even killed us. Sin is like that. If we don't do anything about it, we stay sick on the inside and separated from God; sin eventually destroys us. If we choose to turn to Jesus, He'll deal with our sin and give us life – but it's our choice whether or not to turn to Him.

God's plan is for everyone to be saved, but each person has to choose whether or not they want to go along with His plan.

 Challenge

Do your friends and family know about God's plan? Could you be the person to tell them?

CORE THEME | CREATION 2

Eye for detail

READ: PSALM 8:1–9

KEY VERSE V1
*'Lord, our Lord, how majestic is your name
in all the earth!'*

Over the past couple of weeks we've talked about how
incredible God's creation is. We've mentioned space and
its vastness. We've touched on the staggering detail
and intricacy of the world and the amazing diversity
in the animal kingdom. We've also looked at our own
responsibility to act in a way that looks after creation,
rather than damages it.

But above all, creation points us towards God. The
universe tells us that God is immensely powerful, creative
and surprising. It shows us that He has an incredible eye
for detail. God is the one who created the world, cares for
it and holds it together. What's more, He still creates now,
by bringing life and hope into impossible situations. When
we look at creation, our response should be the same as
the writer of this psalm. Verses 3–4 put it like this: 'When I
consider your heavens, the work of your fingers, the moon
and the stars, which you have set in place, what is mankind
that you are mindful of them?' David was quite simply
blown away by what he saw around him. Let's follow
his example and worship God for being so wonderful,
powerful and creative.

Pray

*Take some time to worship God now. Thank Him for the beauty
of creation and praise Him for being amazing. Why not sit in
your garden or go for a walk in a park to get inspiration?*

CORE THEME | CREATION 2

Creative creator

READ: GENESIS 1:26–31

KEY VERSE V26
'Then God said, "Let us make mankind in our image, in our likeness"'

In the first section of our series on 'Creation', we talked about how incredible the world is and how amazing God must be for putting it together. During the next week, we'll investigate how God created us; who we are because of that; and how we can use our God-given creativity to worship Him.

The first thing the Bible teaches us about who we are is that God made us to be like Him. This doesn't mean we're perfect, but it does mean that we have the ability to show love, wisdom, justice and truth, just as God does. So, we should do what we can to show those qualities. Let's also keep in mind that the people around us are made in God's image too. Because of that, we must respect them – even if we don't like them. Also, when God says, 'Let us make human beings in our image', it shows that we're made in the image of God the Father, Jesus and the Holy Spirit. God models relationship by being three persons in one God. In the same way, we're created to be in meaningful relationships with other people and with God. We're not supposed to go through life all on our own.

And one final thing: if God the creator made us to be like Him, surely that means we are naturally creative too. In the next few days, we'll think about what that might mean.

CORE THEME | CREATION 2

Think

How will knowing that other people are made in God's image affect how you treat them?

Uniquely you

READ: PSALM 139:1–18

KEY VERSE V13
'For you created my inmost being; you knit me together in my mother's womb.'

When you were a kid, did you ever enjoy putting together Airfix kits? (Just in case you've never experienced the joy of an Airfix kit, it includes many pieces of plastic, which, when put together properly, form a scale model of an aircraft, ship etc.) It is quite an intricate and fiddly thing to do. You can easily end up with lumps of glue all over the model or parts stuck on in slightly the wrong place. Then you have to paint the model with a very steady hand. By the time you are finished, the model will hopefully look like an aeroplane, but maybe not exactly like the picture on the box. Unless you are very good at this sort of thing, you may end up feeling a bit disappointed with the final result.

Fortunately, God doesn't work like this. He isn't clumsy and doesn't make mistakes. When He puts each of us together, He takes care, and He knows every last detail about us. And unlike the Airfix kit, God doesn't need to copy a picture on a box. He uses incredible variety in creating our looks, our skills and our personalities. God loves each of us so much that He makes each of us completely unique – a one-off, never to be repeated.

 Pray

Creator God, thank You for making me, me! Thank You for caring about even the smallest details of who I am. Thank You for loving me enough to make me completely unique. Amen.

CORE THEME | CREATION 2

Weekend

30 JUN/1 JUL

The future's so bright

READ: JEREMIAH 1:4–10

KEY VERSE V5
'Before I formed you in the womb I knew you'

God knows you better than anyone else in the world does. In fact, He even knows you better than you know yourself. Before you were born, before your mum realised she was pregnant, before God even started putting you together, He knew everything about you. When life gets hard, when other people just don't seem to understand us, isn't it comforting and reassuring to know that God loves us, created us and knows us inside out?

What's more, God has plans for you. In verse 5 God says to Jeremiah, 'before you were born I set you apart; appointed you as a prophet to the nations'. Isn't that amazing? And because

He knows you so well, His plans for you are perfect. Maybe you have reached a stage in your life where you are starting to think about what you are going to do with it. Or maybe there is something that you have wanted to do or be from an early age. God creates each of us with different skills and personalities and, if we stick to God's plans, we can use our skills and personalities to achieve brilliant things for Him.

Sometimes God will ask us to do things that we may feel we are not equipped to do or that scare us. For example, Jeremiah's job was to tell his countrymen that they'd turned away from God and to warn them that they were heading for severe consequences because of that! His initial response was, 'I can't speak for you! I'm too young!' But God reassured Jeremiah by reminding him that He would be with Him. God will never ask us to do something that we can't do, with His help. And, whatever happens, the God who knows you, created you and loves you is always with you (v8).

➕ *Challenge*

Ask your church leader about using your skills and talents at church – maybe as a welcomer, musician or contributing to the church newsletter or website?

New life

READ: 2 CORINTHIANS 5:14–18

KEY VERSE V17
'if anyone is in Christ, the new creation has come: the old has gone, the new is here!'

It's your first day at school. Your shirt is spotless. Your tie is neat. Your shoes are shiny. How long does your uniform stay that way? After a day or two of running around in the playground, spilling your dinner, enjoying messy art lessons and generally fooling around, you're likely to look a bit grubby. Your mum or dad do the best they can to get the muck out of your shirt, polish your shoes and undo the knots in your tie, but your actions have had an effect. You can only really look smart again if you get a new uniform!

When God created humans He made us in His image – excellent! But there was a problem. We messed up. And the selfish choices we make now take us away from God. It's as though our lives get covered in muck that makes it impossible for us to get close to a holy and spotless God. God's solution is amazing. He doesn't try to clean up our old life. He gives us a new one! Because Jesus died and rose again, we can receive His new life. If we follow Jesus, our old life is dead, but we get an exciting, fresh, new life instead. God doesn't just create us once. If we give Him control of our lives, He recreates us.

CORE THEME | CREATION 2

🔅 Think

Do you feel you have made a mess in an area of your life? Ask God to show you where you might be in need of His help. God promises that if we ask for forgiveness, He will forgive us and make us clean again because He loves us so much.

Gifts from heaven

READ: JAMES 1:16–18

KEY VERSE V17
*'Every good and perfect gift is from above, coming
down from the Father of the heavenly lights'*

What are you thankful for? Your iPad? That new pair of
shoes? The school holidays coming up? Or perhaps life's
not good at the moment. Maybe you have fallen out with
friends, someone you know is ill or you have some tough
tests coming up at school. Sometimes we can find it
difficult to think of anything to be thankful for. However, if
we really think about it, we all have loads to be thankful
for, however we feel. Just having somewhere to live, food
to eat and clothes to wear are huge blessings – so many of
us have much more than that. Families, friends, health and
opportunity for an education – the list goes on, and most
of us will have all of these.

It's important to be grateful for the good things we have,
but it's also important to remember where these things
come from. Anything that's good comes from God. He's
the creator of 'the heavenly lights' and the provider of
everything good, and He always will be. He's been a creator
and provider from the beginning, and He doesn't change.
Because He loves us so much, He keeps creating good
things and providing them for us. Anything we have that's
good is a gift from the God who loves us, which includes
the Bible, 'his true word'.

Challenge
*Make a list of all the good things in your life. Then thank
God for each of these things.*

CORE THEME | CREATION 2

Deep roots

READ: LAMENTATIONS 3:19–24

KEY VERSE V23
'Great is his faithfulness; his mercies begin afresh each morning.' (NLT)

The Mojave Desert, located in the southwestern United States, is one of the most inhospitable places on the planet. Temperatures there can reach up to 56°C and in the driest years rainfall can be less than five centimetres a year (compared to up to 50 metres a year in parts of Britain). And yet, this hostile environment is the only place on the planet in which you will find the Joshua tree. The tree's unique shape reminded early settlers of Joshua (in the Bible) reaching his hands up to the sky in prayer. Despite the extreme heat and lack of water, the Joshua tree thrives there. How is this possible? It's because of the tree's deep and extensive root system. The Joshua tree's roots can grow up to 11 metres long in order to find water deep underground. Because the roots are deep enough, the tree can thrive in a seriously harsh environment.

What helps you thrive when life seems harsh? If your roots are deep into God, He can keep you strong and growing, however hot things get. Even if everything else looks bleak, one thing never changes. God is with us. He is faithful, and His love and mercy never run out. Whatever happens, you can always trust God to love you and stay with you.

 Pray

Lord, thank You that Your love and mercy are new every morning. Help me to grow deep roots into You, so that I'll stay strong. Amen.

CORE THEME | CREATION 2

Great skills

READ: EXODUS 31:1–11

KEY VERSE V6
'I have given ability to all the skilled workers to make everything I have commanded you'

Eric Liddell was a gifted athlete and passionate about sport. At the 1924 Olympics, he won a gold medal in the 400 metres and a bronze in the 200 metres. On his return to his native Scotland, Eric was hailed as a hero. Eric was passionate about running, but he was also passionate about following Jesus. And there were some who were surprised at his interest in athletics. Surely running was just frivolous – a waste of time for a man who wanted to live as a Christian? Eric answered his critics simply: 'I believe God made me for a purpose, but He also made me fast! And when I run I feel His pleasure.'

God creates each of us with unique skills and abilities. For Eric Liddell, this meant an ability to run fast. Think about the skills God has given you. Perhaps you're great at science or gifted in music or languages. Maybe God's simply made you wise. If God's created you with a skill, it's important to use it. For a start, it's a way of saying 'Thank You' to God for what He's given you. Also, when we use our gifts, it points other people towards God. Eric Liddell made it clear that God had made him fast.

We shouldn't be embarrassed to use our God-given abilities. In fact, it brings Him glory when we use what He's given us.

Think

What skills has God given you? How can you use your skills to point other people towards Him?

CORE THEME | CREATION 2

Good ambassadors

READ: COLOSSIANS 3:16–17

KEY VERSE V17
'whatever you do or say, do it as a representative of the Lord Jesus' (NLT)

An ambassador represents his home country, while living in another nation. He communicates his country's interests to the country in which he currently lives, and whatever he says or does reflects on his home country. Of course, this is a big responsibility not to be taken lightly. If the ambassador says or does something carelessly, everyone will think less of his home country because of his thoughtless deed or word. But it's a real opportunity too. If the ambassador relates well to the people around him and handles difficult situations skilfully, it makes his country look good and really improves the relationship between the two nations.

Today's verses tell us that we're Jesus' ambassadors. We represent Jesus to the people around us. (Remember, Genesis 1:26 tells us that we're created to be like Jesus too.) This is a responsibility, because everything we say and do reflects on Jesus and on fellow Christians. But it's an amazing opportunity too. If we speak and act remembering that we're ambassadors of Jesus, anything we do can be an act of worship to Him and show other people how great He is. Whether we're studying, dancing, playing football or doing the washing up, we can do all these things in a way that brings glory to God.

CORE THEME | CREATION 2

 ## Challenge
How can you be an ambassador for Jesus at school, home or college?

**WEEKEND
7/8 JUL**

DATING

Love is powerful

READ: 1 CORINTHIANS 13:1–13

KEY VERSE V4
'Love is patient, love is kind. It does not envy, it does not boast, it is not proud.'

Back in May, we started to explore the topic of dating and what the Bible might have to say on this relatively modern phenomenon. We have found that God designed us to be in relationship with others, romantic or otherwise, and that He wants to guide us in handling those relationships wisely. Another key theme we can draw from the Bible is that God shows us how to love others. If we want to know how best to love other people, then the Bible has a lot to tell us. In the next fortnight we will focus on how we can ensure that we behave in a loving and God-honouring way, particularly in romantic relationships.

Love is powerful. Not only does it have the power to deeply affect our emotions, but our love can have a profound, even physical, effect on others. Very occasionally there are instances where stillborn babies have come back to life. As the parents have been cradling the seemingly lifeless child in their arms to say their last goodbyes, incredibly the baby starts to breathe and show signs of life. The loving words and touch of the parents have stirred the baby's vital organs to begin working. Of course, at the many times where this does not happen, it does not mean that the baby was not dearly loved.

If you've ever been to a church wedding, then the chances are that you've heard the verses in today's passage before. These words reiterate that love is powerful. They also make us stop and reflect on what actions are loving. Think for a few minutes about the people who love you. How do you know that they love you?

Think

How do you show love to those around you? Do you need to make more effort in this? How can you take on Paul's words in 1 Corinthians 13 and act on them?

Use responsibly

READ: ECCLESIASTES 7:26

KEY VERSE V26
*'I discovered that a seductive woman is a trap more
bitter than death. Her passion is a snare'* (NLT)

When you thought yesterday about different ways in
which people express love, did you think of any physical
expressions of love? Physical affection is one of those
important ways we show our love for others. Right from the
start of life, a baby experiences their parents' love from how
they are held. Babies who are starved of this loving touch
are apparently seriously disadvantaged. Their physical and
mental development may be stunted because of it.

Perhaps the ultimate physical expression of love
is 'making love' (or sex). Some people seem to get the
impression that sex is in some way inherently bad. But this
is not the case! In fact, sex is part of God's creation – He
invented it! So, why is sex sometimes talked about as if it is
dangerous, such as in today's key verse?

Think about fire. It has a lot of valuable and important
uses. It is not essentially bad. However, imagine you find
a small child playing with fire. You would, quite rightly, be
very worried. Most toddlers are not capable of using fire
responsibly. In the wrong hands, fire becomes dangerous.
We could say the same thing about sex. It's good, important
and very enjoyable, but if we use it irresponsibly, we can
easily get hurt, and hurt others.

 Pray
*Thank God for the gift of sex. Ask for His wisdom in using
this gift in the way He intended.*

HOT TOPIC | DATING 2

Don't get burnt

READ: 1 THESSALONIANS 4:3–8

KEY VERSE V3
'God's will is for you to be holy, so stay away from all sexual sin.' (NLT)

Yesterday we explored the idea that sex is good but can also be dangerous. Most Christians therefore see sex as best saved for marriage. Probably the next question is, 'How far is too far in a dating relationship?' Or is that looking at it the wrong way? When we ask the question, 'How far is too far?' maybe what we're really asking is, 'How far can I go before I'm in trouble with God?'

Would you soak your left arm in petrol to see how close you could get it to a bonfire before it caught light? Probably not! But when it comes to sex we ask, 'How far is too far? How far can I go without getting burned?'

God's will is for us to be holy in every area of our lives. He wants us to be pure and godly, even when that goes against what everyone else seems to be doing. As part of this, God wants us to stay away from sexual sin. So, rather than asking how far it is OK to go in our physical relationships, perhaps we should be asking, 'How can I stay pure and honour God in this relationship?'

Think
Are you trying to push the boundaries rather than aiming to live in a pure and holy way? Do you need to change your attitude on this? Is there anything you need to say sorry to God for, and receive His forgiveness?

Set boundaries

READ: SONG OF SONGS 2:1–17

KEY VERSE V7
*'Promise me, O women of Jerusalem... not to awaken
love until the time is right.' (NLT)*

HOT TOPIC | DATING 2

Most people who haven't read a lot of the Bible would
probably perceive it to be anti-sex. But this is certainly
not the case! Song of Songs uses a lot of imagery but,
even so, it is not difficult to work out what the gist of it
is. It describes an intense love and attraction between a
man and a woman, with a clear physical element to their
relationship. Having read Song of Songs, we can see that
sex is not inherently wrong; in this context it's good! (In
fact, the couple's expressions of how good it is are enough
to make anyone blush!) However, the book does underline
that there is a right time and place for acting on a physical
attraction.

In today's key verse, we are warned 'not to awaken
love until the time is right' (Songs 2:7). What does that
mean in the physical sense? Well, we need to decide what
boundaries we'll set up in our physical relationships. Ask
yourself what do you want to save for marriage? How
can you honour this person and God with your actions?
Whether or not you are dating somebody at the moment,
these are important things to consider.

 ## *Challenge*

*Working out your boundaries ahead of time will help you
stick to them. What might it mean for you 'not to awaken
love until the time is right'?*

First impressions

READ: PROVERBS 31:10–12,25–31

KEY VERSE V30
'Charm is deceptive, and beauty is fleeting; but a woman who fears the Lord is to be praised.'

Do you enjoy playing practical jokes on your friends? Maybe placing a fake insect in their bag or on their desk. Or replacing the sugar with salt in the sugar bowl at home and seeing if anyone puts salt on their breakfast cereal.

We can often be fooled by first impressions. If you had to define what makes somebody attractive, what would you say? A perfect figure, a confident attitude and stylish clothes will all get people's attention. But what really matters in a person is far deeper than that. Whether you're male or female, it's your character that really counts.

Rather than get carried away with first impressions, take some time to think about what really counts in a boyfriend/girlfriend. What do you have in common with this person? Do you share important values and priorities? Will this person help you to maintain a healthy focus on God and His plans for your life? Is this person attractive on the surface but with an unpleasant personality? Thinking these things through will help you make decisions on potential relationships.

Think

What would God say about what you look for in a potential boyfriend/girlfriend? And on the other hand, what impression do you give other people? Are you more concerned with looking good than with becoming more like Jesus?

HOT TOPIC | DATING 2

77

Real wisdom

READ: PROVERBS 2:12–22

KEY VERSE V16
'Wisdom will save you from the immoral woman, from the seductive words of the promiscuous woman.' (NLT)

In the film *Frozen*, Ana meets the dashing Prince Hans at a ball, falls head-over-heels in love with him, and in the same evening decides she wants to marry him. When Ana tells her sister, Elsa, of her plans, Elsa is stunned at the rapid romance and refuses to give her permission for the marriage to take place. Hugely disappointed at not getting the response she wanted from her sister, Ana continues with the romance regardless.

All too often, we can be like this. We want wise advice from other people, but we want their wisdom to be something that's easy to hear. Proverbs highlights the importance of wisdom in helping us make the right choices about our relationships. Bad decisions in this area of life can have devastating consequences. We need to be disciplined and show real wisdom when it comes to dating. Remember to guard your heart, as it's so easy to get carried away by our emotions. We'll sometimes have to choose between what's right and what's appealing.

Pray

Ask for God's wisdom for making decisions on romantic relationships. Ask Him to help you make the right decision, when the wrong decision is a more attractive option.

HOT TOPIC | DATING 2

Weekend

14/15 JUL

Positive influences

READ: PROVERBS 22:24–25

KEY VERSE V24
'Do not make friends with a hot-tempered person, do not associate with one easily angered'

There is a saying that goes, 'Be careful the friends you choose for you will become like them'. Sometimes there are people we know who bring out the worst in us. When we are around them we may start to feel increasingly tense and grumpy. With others, we may be more inclined than usual to start gossiping! Proverbs 22 reminds us that hanging around with the wrong sort of people can have a negative effect on our own personality. It's so true that when we hang around with someone who is always grumpy and negative, their attitude rubs off on us. This is not to say we shouldn't help someone who is going through a difficult time and whose emotions are obviously impacted by this, but let's try to be aware of the effect others are having on us.

Hopefully there are also people in our lives who bring out the best in us. They encourage us when we're down, challenge us when we are doing the wrong thing and spur us on to serve God and others. They share God's wisdom and truth with us and always look out for our best interests. These are the people who God wants us to be influenced by. And the Holy Spirit is the best influence of all. Galatians 5 tells us that when we allow the Holy Spirit to influence us, He produces 'love, joy, peace, patience, kindness, goodness, faithfulness, gentleness, and self-control' in us (Gal. 5:22–23). The Holy Spirit will not only produce these great traits in us, He will also lead us to the right people and help us deal with those who once influenced us in the wrong way.

Think

If our purpose in life is to know God and live for Him, then we need to look for people who will support us in this. Similarly, are there ways we can support others in their own walk with Jesus? How are you doing with those goals at the moment?

Sleep on it

READ: PSALM 4:1–8

KEY VERSE V4
'Don't sin by letting anger control you. Think about it overnight and remain silent.' (NLT)

Arguments feature in all relationships. In fact, it is something to worry about if you never disagree with someone! What is important is how you deal with your differences when disagreements come up.

Many people home in on the Bible's advice not to let the sun go down on your anger (Eph. 4:26). This is a valuable piece of advice but can, when misinterpreted, lead to more problems. It does not necessarily have to mean getting the whole issue sorted out before you go to sleep. When we are tired late at night, it is easy to become irrational and stress about issues that we wouldn't normally worry about when we are fully rested. Being over-tired makes it very difficult to sort out any arguments. This is where today's verse comes in handy. To let go of our anger does not necessarily mean sorting out the whole issue there and then.

Do your parents tell you that things will look better in the morning? Usually they are right. Things that worry us late at night often seem insignificant once we've had a good night's sleep.

 Pray
Father God, help me to behave in a godly way when I disagree with someone. Help me to be patient and to control my anger. Amen.

HOT TOPIC | DATING 2

Amicable split

READ: GENESIS 13:5–9

KEY VERSE V9
'Take your choice of any section of the land you want, and we will separate.' (NLT)

We have all heard of divorce proceedings that turn nasty, perhaps amongst people we know or celebrities in the news. When Paul McCartney and Heather Mills divorced in 2008, insane allegations were made in order to discredit the other. Paul McCartney said that marrying Heather Mills was his 'biggest mistake'. Whether we like it or not, many of our dating relationships will come to an end. Abram and Lot were uncle and nephew, so certainly weren't in a romantic relationship, but the way in which they parted sets a great example for us.

The disputes had started to break out between Abram and his nephew Lot's people as a result of them 'living so close together' (Gen. 13:6, NLT). Some of us can probably identify with this problem in certain relationships of our own with people we are close to. Eventually, Abram and Lot agree that they have to go their own separate ways. What is remarkable is what Abram does next.

When we split up with someone, we often look out for our own interests in the situation. We want to benefit as much as possible. But this is not Abram's attitude. He allows Lot to choose the land that he prefers, and agrees to accept what is left.

Challenge
In your relationships, particularly when they come to an end, are you out to get the best for yourself? How can you adopt Abram's attitude when a relationship comes to an end?

HOT TOPIC | DATING 2

Think before you speak

READ: GALATIANS 5:13–15

KEY VERSE V15
*'If you bite and devour each other, watch out or you
will be destroyed by each other.'*

It should come as no surprise that God commands us to
love other people. (After all, God Himself is love – 1 John
4:8.) But along with this command come warnings of the
negative consequences when we don't love others in the
way that we should. In your relationships with others, do
you truly love them? Do you build them up to be the best
people they can be? What about when you're arguing?

Today's passage warns us against destroying one
another. However, as well as destroying one another, we
can also do damage to our relationship with God when
we leave issues unresolved. In Matthew 5 we read that we
cannot come before God with a clear conscience if we are
not at peace in our relationships (Matt. 5:23–24).

Conflict is an inevitable part of relationships, but we
must be careful even at these times to ensure we behave
in a godly way and do our best to love the other person.
When we do not deal with issues wisely and behave in
ways we regret, the consequences might be long-lasting.

Think

*Is there somebody with whom you have had a relationship
that ended badly? Are there past hurts that have not
been resolved? Ask God to help you deal with these issues
whether privately in your own heart or by talking things
over with the person involved.*

HOT TOPIC | DATING 2

Great minds think alike

READ: PHILIPPIANS 2:1–5

KEY VERSE V2
'agreeing wholeheartedly with each other, loving one another, and working together with one mind and purpose.' (NLT)

Do you have a sibling or a friend that you know so well that you are able to tell what the other is thinking? You might even be able to finish the other's sentences, because you know exactly what is on the other's mind. Often twins are like this: they have some kind of unusually strong link through their close relationship.

In today's passage, Paul urges us to work 'together with one mind and purpose' (Phil. 2:2, NLT). The Bible describes marriage as a husband and wife becoming 'united into one' (Mark 10:8, NLT). In our relationships, then, we need to have the same focus and be united in our purpose.

We have thought a lot about choosing the right partner and not being led astray by somebody who is not good for us. However, we also need to be concerned with our own actions and behaviour and whether or not we are a good influence on our partner! This passage emphasises the importance of putting others and their needs first. If both parties do that in relationships then each benefits.

Pray
Lord Jesus, thank You that You were willing to humble Yourself and come to earth to save me. Help me to put others' needs before my own. Amen.

HOT TOPIC | DATING 2

The meaning of love

READ: 1 JOHN 4:7–21

KEY VERSE V10
'This is real love—not that we loved God, but that he loved us and sent his Son as a sacrifice to take away our sins.' (NLT)

If you had to try to define love, what would you say? There are several words for love in Ancient Greek, all with slightly different meanings. *Eros* and *agape* are perhaps the two most common and the most relevant for us to consider. *Eros* is a passionate, often physical love. It is from this word that we get our English word 'erotic'. *Agape* could be described as a sacrificial and unconditional love. You could say it is more of a spiritual love than the physical attraction implied by *eros*.

In your definition of love, did you focus more on one of these kinds of love than the other or did they have an equal balance? Would you be happy to have a dating or marriage relationship that only consisted of one of these types of love, or do you think that both are necessary?

In the original Greek of 1 John 4, the word used for 'love' is *agape*. God is the ultimate definition of *agape love*. God calls us to demonstrate *agape* love to everyone, which is a huge challenge to all of us, whether we're in a relationship or not!

✚ Challenge

Spend some time looking back over today's passage and 1 Corinthians 13. Both of these passages give us insights into what agape love looks like. How can you reflect agape love in your own relationships, whether romantic or otherwise? What changes could you make in light of this?

HOT TOPIC | DATING 2

MONEY

Share and share alike

READ: ACTS 2:42–47

KEY VERSE V44
'All the believers were together and had everything in common.'

It seems that every couple of years or so, one country or another (maybe even our own) experiences a recession. The term 'recession' means a period of significant economic decline lasting longer than a few months. It is marked by high unemployment, a freeze on wages and a fall in retail sales, and many people find themselves affected by it. In times of recession, most people are forced to think very carefully about where their money goes, including the different charities and causes that they may give to.

How can we, as Christians, respond to such a crisis? Is it right for us to reduce our giving? How do we support those who are really going through difficult times financially? It has always been the case that some have more than others. And in order to counteract this, the early Christians we read about in today's reading chose to live in community, sharing everything they had so that no one went without.

It might not be possible for us to live in community in quite the same way, but the Bible still gives insight and instruction as to how we should care for each other in hard times. Over the next couple of weeks we're going to be looking at part of a letter that the apostle Paul wrote to the church in Corinth, whose members were also experiencing tough financial circumstances. This church was full of fairly new Christians who still needed to be taught about giving, so Paul gave them some principles that we too can model in our own giving.

Pray

Lord, thank You that You know all that we are going through and the situations in which we find ourselves. Please speak to us about how we can play our part in supporting others. Amen.

Give what you can

☰ **READ: 2 CORINTHIANS 8:1–5**

KEY VERSE V2
'they are very poor. But they are also filled with abundant joy, which has overflowed in rich generosity.' (NLT)

Have you ever heard of the Christmas appeal project called Operation Christmas Child? It is a wonderful idea where a shoebox is packed full with items such as colouring books, paper, toys, toiletries and sweets. The box is wrapped and then is sent to another country where children have very little. The idea is to show God's love in a tangible way to needy children around the world. Even if you do not have very much spare money, this is a fantastic opportunity to make someone very happy.

In this part of his letter, Paul is encouraging the church in Corinth to be generous and is using the example of a church in Macedonia, who were experiencing even more difficult times than the Corinthians. The first principle Paul wants them to grasp is that generosity is possible even when your finances are really stretched, and that it's possible to give with joy, even in these circumstances. In the face of severe affliction and extreme poverty, the Macedonian believers responded with joy. How? Because they recognised that God had been generous to them, so they should extend that to others.

➕ Challenge

Even though it's only July, it's not too early to get involved with Operation Christmas Child! Find an old shoebox and start filling it now with things to donate. More details are on the Samaritan's Purse website.

Excel in giving

READ: 2 CORINTHIANS 8:6–7

KEY VERSE V7
'since you excel in everything... see that you also excel in this grace of giving.'

Are you a Scrooge? In Charles Dickens' novel, *A Christmas Carol*, Scrooge hated parting with his hard-earned money. On Christmas Eve, he turns away two men who are seeking a donation from him in order to provide food and heating for the poor. He is shown the consequences of his actions by three ghosts and three visions. The result is that, by the end of the story, Scrooge has a complete change of heart and begins to treat everyone with kindness, generosity and compassion.

There are many charity organisations trying to get funds using a variety of means such as mail-outs, phone calls or charity workers in shopping centres. Sometimes we might feel pressured into giving away our hard-earned money and want to hang on to it for ourselves.

In 2 Corinthians, Paul acknowledges that giving doesn't always come easily to people. It doesn't feel natural to want to give money away when times are difficult, but he says this is a gift or a 'ministry' to be exercised. He challenges the Corinthians not to just do this a little bit but to really excel in it. His second principle for them to learn is that giving is a spiritual gift – it is something the Holy Spirit can help them to do.

 Think

Are there people you know who have a great gift of giving? Talk to them about what has helped them to be generous.

HOT TOPIC | MONEY 2

Generous like Jesus

READ: 2 CORINTHIANS 8:8–9

KEY VERSE V9
*'though he [Jesus] was rich, yet for your sake he
became poor, so that you through his poverty might
become rich.'*

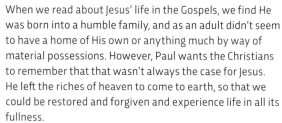

When we read about Jesus' life in the Gospels, we find He
was born into a humble family, and as an adult didn't seem
to have a home of His own or anything much by way of
material possessions. However, Paul wants the Christians
to remember that that wasn't always the case for Jesus.
He left the riches of heaven to come to earth, so that we
could be restored and forgiven and experience life in all its
fullness.

Paul reminds his readers of the generosity that Jesus
showed to them and to us all, both through His life and
His death. So when we are generous to others, we remind
ourselves and others of Jesus' generosity. Paul tells us:
'Don't do this because you have to. Do it because you want
to, because you know that is how God has treated you.'

In a letter to another church, the church in Philippi, Paul
picks up this theme and tells us that we should have the
same attitude as Jesus. And when we are generous with
others, they will be reminded of Him (Phil. 2:5–11).

Pray
*Thank You, Lord, that You gave up the riches of heaven
to come and live on earth and to die on the cross to pay
my debt. Please let my life reflect my thankfulness to You.
Amen.*

HOT TOPIC | MONEY 2

Give within your means

 READ: 2 CORINTHIANS 8:10-12

KEY VERSE V12
'For if the willingness is there, the gift is acceptable according to what one has, not according to what one does not have.'

Paul's fourth principle is incredibly practical and immensely freeing! We can be so tempted to compare ourselves to others in a whole number of areas that we forget that God sees us as individuals and knows the situation we are in.

Having you ever gone on a shopping trip with a friend who has more spending money than you? You might be tempted to buy the same items that your friend does even though you have a different budget. It is difficult to stay disciplined in these circumstances and not over-spend.

We all have different amounts of resources available to us, and God doesn't expect us all to give the same. What He is interested in is our heart: are we generous with what we have? Or are we stingy and wanting to hold on to it all for ourselves? Paul's advice to the Corinthians links back to the passage we looked at a few weeks ago about the poor widow who gave just a couple of pennies. In Jesus' eyes she gave much more than the rich people, because to Jesus it's not the amount that matters, it's our willingness to give cheerfully, even when that hurts.

HOT TOPIC | MONEY 2

 Challenge
Do you give regularly to a charity or to your church? Try to develop a good habit of giving regularly, even if it is only a small amount.

A golden opportunity

READ: 2 CORINTHIANS 8:13–15

KEY VERSE V14
'Right now you have plenty and can help those who are in need. Later, they will have plenty and can share with you when you need it.' (NLT)

Within the Church of England, there is something called the 'Common Fund'. Congregations in every parish (area) around the country give their share which is collected and placed into the fund. It is then redistributed equally to every church to provide and support clergy and further the Church's work. This method means that all churches can share resources fairly. By giving sacrificially and generously, wealthier churches can support poorer churches.

This is the principle that Paul is encouraging in this passage where he says, 'I only mean that there should be some equality' (v13). At that moment the church in Corinth had more resources than churches in other places, but the time would come when it would be the other way around. When we have plenty, we have an ideal opportunity to bless others. Not only is this a perfect way to show love by giving and helping others, but maybe there will come a time in the future when we also will need help.

 Think

Where in the world is there a need that you know of? How could you use what you have plenty of, to help with this need? Or closer to home, is there a simple way you could show generosity to your friends – for example, sharing food when you have cooked or bought too much?

HOT TOPIC | MONEY 2

Weekend

Honour your promises

READ: 2 CORINTHIANS 9:1–5

KEY VERSE V2
'For I know your eagerness to help... and your enthusiasm has stirred most of them to action.'

Are you competitive in your family? Some siblings are incredibly competitive with each other. If one learns how to play the guitar, the other has to learn how to do it better. If one sibling can swim 20 lengths, the other has to swim 50. The competition can sometimes lead to a certain amount of friction in relationships. But competition isn't always a bad thing; it can sometimes be the spur to do more than we thought we could.

Paul is encouraging the Corinthians in a level of healthy competition with the church in Macedonia, and reminds them that it was because the Macedonians were so inspired by their generosity that they themselves started giving. However, it now seemed that the Macedonians were out-giving the Corinthians and Paul was anxious that the Corinthians wouldn't forget the promise of support that they had made to the church in Jerusalem.

Paul appeals to their pride, pointing out how embarrassing it would be if he were to arrive in Corinth with some people from Macedonia, to collect their gift and take it on to the church in Jerusalem, only to find that they didn't have it ready. He really wanted them to honour their promises of support.

Challenge

What's the most generous thing anyone has ever done for you? How could you pay that generosity forward to someone else? It doesn't have to be to the same scale, but think about what you can afford, and who you can bless.

Invest wisely

READ: 2 CORINTHIANS 9:6–7

KEY VERSE V7
'Each of you should give what you have decided in your heart to give, not reluctantly or under compulsion, for God loves a cheerful giver.'

Depending on where you live, you might get a lot of people 'cold-calling' at your front door. People from all sorts of different charities can turn up at your door, asking you to sign up to give £2 a month to support some project or other. Some of them will even tell you how wonderful your neighbours have been in signing up. You might feel under pressure to give the person on the doorstep what they want, but may not be particularly cheerful about it.

Paul is keen that the Corinthians don't find themselves in that place. He says that we should make our own minds up about how much we will give and then do that cheerfully. However, Paul wants them to be aware that the farming principle of 'you reap what you sow' also applies to how we use our money. So, just as you will reap a harvest of tomatoes if you plant tomatoes, if you sow generously you will receive generously. You will see a harvest of people's lives being changed as a result of your generosity. That is something to get really excited about.

Think

Take some time to review the work of a few charities and find out what it is they are raising money for. Is this something you could invest in cheerfully?

HOT TOPIC | MONEY 2

Standard of giving

READ: 2 CORINTHIANS 9:8–10

KEY VERSE V8
*'And God will generously provide all you need. Then
you will always have everything you need and plenty
left over to share with others.' (NLT)*

John Wesley was a famous preacher whom God used to
bring thousands of people to faith in eighteenth-century
England. Wesley is also known as the man who started
the Methodist Church. His name is very well known in
Christian circles, but not many people know that Wesley
made a lot of money from preaching.

One cold winter's day, he was very challenged by God
about how he used his money. He had bought new pictures
for his home and had just finished paying for them when
the maid arrived, wearing only a thin dress. Wesley wanted
to give her some money to buy a coat, but realised that he
didn't have any left. From that point on, he resolved to live
on £28 a year, no matter how much he earned, and give
the rest away. He believed that with increasing income, it
shouldn't be a Christian's standard of living that improves,
but their standard of giving. Wesley encouraged other
Christians to gain all the money they could, so they could
do good with it. He also encouraged them to buy only what
they really needed. When we buy what we don't need, we
then want more things that we don't need. When he died,
the only money Wesley had was the change in his pocket.

 Challenge

**This week, rather than spending money on something for
yourself, could you buy something for someone in need?**

HOT TOPIC | MONEY 2

Changing motivations

 **READ: 2 CORINTHIANS 9:11–13**

KEY VERSE V13
'they will give glory to God. For your generosity to
them... will prove that you are obedient to the Good
News of Christ.' (NLT)

For Paul, everything is linked. The way we behave is clearly
linked to what we believe. If we believe that God has been
generous to us and has given us all things, then we will be
quick to be generous to others. We will recognise that all
that we have belongs to God and we are simply looking
after it for Him.

Martin Luther is quoted as having said that the last
part of a person to be converted is their wallet! As we get
closer to God and grow in our faith, we will find that our
tight grip on money, possessions and other things starts to
loosen. Along with this, we will find our motives changing.
Whereas we may once have been driven to get as much as
we could for ourselves and reluctant to share with others,
as the Holy Spirit works in our lives we will find that we
want to use what we have to bless others. Paul says this
is an indication that we have really understood the good
news of Jesus and are living it out. And when we live in this
way, it is really pleasing to God because it proves that we
are becoming more like Him.

HOT TOPIC | MONEY 2

 Pray
*God, You have given me so many good things, and most of
all You have given Jesus so that I could know You. Please
make me more and more like You. Amen.*

Worth the sacrifice

≡ **READ: 2 CORINTHIANS 9:14**

KEY VERSE V14
'And in their prayers for you their hearts will go out to you, because of the surpassing grace God has given you.'

→ What we do with our money and possessions has the potential for far-reaching effects. Believe it or not, it's often true that the more we are willing to let go, the more we receive. This doesn't always mean receiving more money, but as we give, God will often bless us in other ways. Apart from anything else, we have the privilege of becoming part of God's work in building His kingdom.

Kisses from Katie* is a biography of a young woman who moved to Uganda when she was just 19 years old, and by the age of 22 had adopted 14 Ugandan children. In the world's eyes, she had given up a good life, a secure future, her education and so much more. Yet, as you read her story, you can't help but be struck by how rich her life sounded: not rich in terms of money and possessions, but rich in people who loved her and in terms of seeing God at work in the people around her.

It's a unique joy to see God transforming people as we invest our time and energy in them. This kind of investment often means we have to sacrifice our own interests, but it can change people's lives, not just in the here and now, but for eternity.

➕ ## Challenge
Over this coming weekend, read a biography of someone who has given up a comfortable life for the sake of the kingdom of God. Reflect on what you can learn from them.

HOT TOPIC | MONEY 2

*Katie Davis, *Kisses from Katie* (New York, USA: Simon & Schuster, 2012)

Best present ever

READ: 2 CORINTHIANS 9:15

KEY VERSE V15
'Thanks be to God for his indescribable gift!'

Who doesn't love Christmas and birthdays? The gifts – both receiving them and giving them. It is lovely to see the way people's faces light up as they respond to gifts that have been carefully chosen for them. Similarly, we can feel incredibly thankful for the thought and effort that people have put into getting gifts for us. Gifts are a key part of our lives but really shouldn't just be reserved for Christmas and birthdays. God has given us a wonderful gift in His Son, Jesus, and it's through Him that we can live to serve God and serve others.

As we come to the end of this part of Paul's letter, he really wants the church in Corinth, and us, to understand that because we have received so much from God, we can be people who love to freely give to others. When we know the truth of the extent of God's love for us, we find things change in us. Our identity and status are no longer found in what we own or in how much money we have; it all becomes about God. Our attitude towards those things changes, not because God says it must, but because it's a natural overflow of His goodness to us.

HOT TOPIC | MONEY 2

Think

Go back over the last two weeks' readings and remind yourself of the principles that Paul sets out about how we think about and use money. How will you put these principles into action?

**WEEKEND
4/5 AUG**

APOLOGETICS

Silent prayers

READ: ROMANS 8:18–30

KEY VERSE V26
'We do not know what we ought to pray for, but Spirit himself intercedes for us through wordless groans.'

In May 2017, a shrapnel-laden bomb was detonated in Manchester Arena killing 23 people and injuring many more. Later the same year, there were other attacks on London Bridge and Borough Market. We see appalling images on our television screens of the aftermath of these sad events; the destruction that the terrorists have inflicted. Families of victims are grief-stricken and stunned as they come to terms with what has happened. Sometimes it is difficult to take in what we are seeing. We want to help but where could we start? There are many practical things we can do, for example donating to a particular charity that helps victims. But one way we can all help is through prayer.

There are times when praying seems incredibly difficult. When we're faced with a tragedy on a personal or even global scale, words often fail us. It's comforting to know that the Holy Spirit prays with us and for us, even in the most extreme circumstances. Through Him, God hears the prayers in our hearts, even if we can't articulate those words. Prayer isn't about saying the right words in the right way. It's just about being honest with God about how we're feeling and what's going on in our lives. It's about a relationship with our Father God who created us and loves us. The Holy Spirit helps us to draw closer to God, even when we can't say a word. People often ask whether prayer achieves anything. Maybe that's missing the point. The most important thing about prayer is simply being with God.

Pray

Spend time with God, being honest about how you're doing and what's on your mind. Don't say a word if you don't want to. Just enjoy being with your heavenly Father.

Unannswered prayers

READ: JAMES 5:13–18

KEY VERSE V16
'The prayer of a righteous person is powerful and effective.'

Imagine the following scenario – there are two married couples, both desperate for a baby but having real trouble conceiving. Both couples pray. But nothing happens. They keep on praying. Still nothing. One couple even starts thinking about getting some medical help in the conception process. They are just about to make a decision when they discover they are pregnant. They are over the moon!

The other couple carry on praying for their miracle baby but nothing happens. They keep on praying. Still nothing. They're really wrestling with this situation now. They're still praying, obviously, but also beginning to wonder whether, for reasons they don't understand, God isn't going to bless them with a baby.

From the first couple's experiences, we can see that God can and does answer our prayers. From the second couple's experiences, it's clear that it doesn't always happen like that. We have no idea why. As we struggle with unanswered prayers, we can only remind ourselves that God is infinitely wise and has reasons beyond our understanding. If we choose to trust Him completely, even when life doesn't make sense, we can be in no better place.

Think

Why do you think God doesn't give us everything we ask for? Think about it and let it lead you into prayer, asking for God's wisdom.

What is truth?

READ: JOHN 8:31–47

KEY VERSE VV31–32
'Jesus said, "If you hold to my teaching, you are really my disciples. Then you will know the truth, and the truth will set you free."'

Truth can be a bit of a slippery thing. These days, people are happy that what you believe can be 'true for you', while at the same time believing something entirely different themselves. So when Christians claim that Jesus is the truth and that He is true for everyone, we often get a frosty response.

Some truth is objective. To take a very extreme example, we all know that the Holocaust happened. There is overwhelming evidence of it, including the experiences of people who survived the death camps. You can't argue that the Holocaust didn't happen and expect to be told, 'Well, that's true for you'. It's a historical fact.

On the other hand, some would argue that chocolate is the best ice cream flavour. That would be true for them. But then other people might think that strawberry is the best flavour. That's true for them and it would be very hard to convince them otherwise. It's just a matter of opinion.

Jesus isn't an ice cream. It's not a matter of Him being true for some of us but not others. Jesus made claims about Himself which demand that we choose whether we believe in Him or not. He's either the Son of God or He isn't. It can't be true for me but not for you.

HOT TOPIC | APOLOGETICS 2

 Challenge

Jesus promises that the truth will set us free, but only if we faithfully follow His teaching. So... are you faithfully following His teaching?

103

Judge not

READ: MATTHEW 7:1–5

KEY VERSE V1
'Do not judge, or you too will be judged.'

It's so sad to hear someone say they'd love to come to church, but they need to 'sort themselves out' first. Somehow, we're giving people the impression that they need to have every little issue in their lives sorted out before they're acceptable – either to God or to us. Somewhere along the line, we've got ourselves a reputation for being judgmental; for pouncing on shortcomings in other people's lives, while showing no concern for our own weaknesses.

In some cases, this might be down to guilt people feel when doing things they know are wrong. Or perhaps we live in a way that's so obviously godly that others feel they can't measure up to that. Maybe. But whether we like it or not, there are a lot of people who have been judged, criticised and gossiped about by Christians and who have been left angry at us and angry at God because of it. If we have a reputation for being judgmental, we've done a fair amount to deserve it. So, if we want to win over people who don't yet know Jesus, we need to be willing to admit our previous failings in showing God's grace.

Think

How can we show God's grace and acceptance to other people, even if we don't approve of how they behave? How can we be intolerant of sin but unconditionally accepting of people?

Have fun God's way

READ: JOHN 10:1–16

KEY VERSE V10
'The thief comes only to steal and kill and destroy; I have come that they may have life, and have it to the full.'

Another common complaint about Christianity is that it limits our freedom. God is often thought of as an almighty killjoy who just wants to stop us enjoying ourselves. Nothing could be further from the truth. Jesus assures us that His purpose is to give us a 'rich and satisfying life'. Yes, that includes life after death, but it starts here and now.

If you're a Christian, you're free to stay up all night, do a bungee jump, visit China, get married, see an amazing film, talk to a stranger, ride a horse, climb a mountain, jump off a waterfall, have kids, sip coke while watching the sun go down over the Zambezi River, have a Christmas dinner in June and cycle the length of the British Isles. Following Jesus can and should be an adventure. Yes, there are a few experiences God doesn't want us to have – promiscuous sex, drinking too much and taking drugs, for example – but that's not because He wants to spoil our fun. The things God warns us away from will ultimately harm us if we pursue them.

Think

Do you miss opportunities because you're naturally cautious? Pray about it, then take a chance and have an adventure. Or do you rush into risky situations because you're impulsive? Ask God to help you be a little wiser.

HOT TOPIC | APOLOGETICS 2

Forgiving reputation

READ: PSALM 103:1–13

KEY VERSE V8
'*the LORD is compassionate and gracious, slow to anger, abounding in love.*'

HOT TOPIC | APOLOGETICS 2

Westboro 'Baptist Church' are notorious for being about the most unforgiving, ungracious 'Christians' in the world. Based in Topeka, Kansas, members of the church picket the funerals of gay people and soldiers, pronouncing God's judgment on them in incredibly harsh terms. They don't stop there, either. Jews, Muslims and even Sweden have been targeted with Westboro's abuse. Tragically enough, they believe they are on a mission to spread 'God's hate'. Quite rightly, they are monitored by the Anti-Defamation League.

But before we start feeling smug because we're not as unforgiving as those guys, just spend a minute thinking about the last person who really let you down. Have you forgiven them? Not easy, is it? C.S. Lewis once pointed out that everyone says forgiveness is a lovely idea until they have something to forgive. But although it's far from easy, forgiveness is God's way. In the same way that God has forgiven us, we're called to forgive other people. The best way to counter the view that Christians are unforgiving is, with God's help, to become known for your gracious, forgiving attitude.

Pray
Ask God to help you forgive. Pray for anyone who's let you down badly and ask for God's help in forgiving them in particular.

Weekend

11/12 AUG

Tricky subjects

READ: LEVITICUS 18:15–30

KEY VERSE V22
'Do not have sexual relations with a man as one does with a woman; that is detestable.'

This verse from Leviticus tends to provoke strong reactions, and is a perfect example of how we shouldn't take single verses out of context without interpreting them within the broader context of Scripture. This verse is often highlighted by those who claim Christians are intolerant. For example, the actor Sir Ian McKellen has admitted to tearing this page out of Bibles when he has stayed in hotels, because he felt it was so out of touch with his lifestyle and culture.

On the other extreme, this is the 'go-to' verse for Christians who are outspoken against homosexual behaviour. The thing is, if we oppose homosexual practice based on this single verse, we haven't got a case. Leviticus forbids homosexuality alongside wearing clothes made of two different fabrics (see 13 June). If one verse holds true, then so should the other. But, as with any other tricky subject in the Bible, we need to make sure we consider the broad sweep of what the Bible has to say, from the creation account in Genesis to the writings about homosexual activity in the New Testament.

The Bible seems to be pretty clear and consistent in outlining that homosexual activity wasn't part of God's original and perfect plan for humanity – and God never lays down 'instructions' for us that aren't for our own benefit in the long run. What the Bible is even clearer about, however, is that we are to treat all people with kindness and respect. There's no place for judgment and hatred. There are lots of tricky subjects in life that need addressing, and will be open for debate within the Christian community, and we need to be open to discussing them with grace and gentleness. Whatever our conclusions, let's make sure they are Bible-based and loving. Remember – it is possible to disagree with someone, and still be their friend!

+ Challenge

Read for yourself what the Bible has to say about homosexuality, and ask God to guide your thinking.

Church makeover

READ: JAMES 4:1–12

KEY VERSE V1
'What causes fights and quarrels among you? Don't they come from your desires that battle within you?'

It's really sad when people accuse the Church of being abusive and controlling. A lot of people seem to like Jesus but have a real problem with 'organised religion' – and they may have a point. Unfortunately, it's easy for churches to become riddled with 'fights and quarrels' over petty issues. And there are churches where people may feel awkward about expressing an opinion that differs to those in leadership.

This is not the way it should be. Churches are full of people, and people are not perfect! So some disagreements and personality clashes *will* happen. But we should strive to be united under God, to put our selfish agendas to one side, serve one another and pursue God's kingdom. One day, the Church will be made perfect, just as the people in it are made perfect. In the meantime, it's a good idea not to judge the Church just because it's a little rough around the edges. God sees the Church as the Bride of Christ – something beautiful. So let's commit ourselves to being part of the Bride's makeover – doing everything we can to help the Church become more beautiful.

HOT TOPIC | APOLOGETICS 2

➕ Challenge
Think of one thing you can do to serve the Church and make it more beautiful. Talk to your friends at church and your church leader. Then put your idea into practice.

A dirty word

 READ: PSALM 51:1–19

KEY VERSE V1
'Have mercy on me, O God, according to your unfailing love; according to your great compassion blot out my transgressions.'

Nobody talks about sin anymore. 'Sin' seems to be anachronistic – a concept that has no place in the twenty-first-century world. Perhaps that's because the word sounds judgmental and people don't like the idea that they should be answerable to someone for how they behave. Nobody wants to be told what to do or that how they're behaving is wrong in some way.

The trouble is our actions have consequences. Whether or not we like being told what to do, the way we behave has an impact on the world and the people around us. We can probably all think of occasions when our actions have hurt someone else, even on purpose. This, really, is what sin is. Sin means a stubborn commitment to independence and putting ourselves first and central in everything, ignoring how it will affect other people and what God might have to say about it all. That's something that has been true of all people, everywhere, throughout time – and is likely to continue to be true forever. We're all guilty of ignoring God and hurting other people and for that reason we all need God's forgiveness.

 Pray

Ask God to forgive you for your sins. If you can think of anything specific you've done which hurt someone else, pray about that in particular. Receive God's forgiveness and pray that people you know will experience this forgiveness too.

HOT TOPIC | APOLOGETICS 2

Final arbiter

READ: ISAIAH 64:1–7

KEY VERSE V6
'All of us have become like one who is unclean, and all our righteous acts are like filthy rags'

You might have heard someone say, 'You don't need to be religious to be good.' Well, let's unpack that. For a start what does 'good' mean? In order to be 'good', you need someone to decide what sort of behaviour is truly 'good' or 'evil' – someone to act as an ultimate moral authority. If we take God out of the equation, we're setting ourselves up as that authority. That is, we decide for ourselves what is good or evil and then behave in line with our own moral choices. Obviously there is a flaw with this line of thinking. What if one person's view of what's 'good' is different to another's? Who's right? Who gets to decide whether a person's actions are truly good? Who has the right to say that? And what's to stop us from altering these views of good and evil to justify doing something wrong?

In the end, it's impossible to live a 'good' life without acknowledging God as the authority on what 'good' means. He is the one who created us, who knows us better than we know ourselves and who is wise enough to know what is really best for us and for the whole human race.

 ## Challenge

Do you really live as if God is the one who decides what is truly 'good'? How would you explain why you do that, if someone asked?

HOT TOPIC | APOLOGETICS 2

Truth with love

READ: EPHESIANS 4:11–16

KEY VERSE V15

'Instead, speaking the truth in love, we will grow to become in every respect the mature body of him who is the head, that is, Christ.'

Imagine your friend spends £70 on a haircut. They're delighted with their new style, but you think it's hideous. You can see it doesn't suit them at all, and people are starting to laugh at your friend behind their back. So what do you do? Surely you have to tell your friend the truth, so that they can get their hair sorted out. But if you're not careful what you say, you could really upset them and have a major falling-out. Telling the truth is important, but we need to choose our words with care.

While it's crucial that we're ready to stand up for what we believe in, we must be careful about how we do this. It's all too easy to get drawn into logical arguments with people who don't share our beliefs. But the more we argue, the less we communicate God's love to the person we're arguing with. Whatever we think of the person we're debating with, God loves them. So let's not be afraid to share what we believe, but let's also remember to share our faith with love. Let's discuss it in a way that shows other people that God loves them – whether they believe in Him or not.

Think

Who do you know who needs to hear about God? How can you share this with them while also showing them that God loves them?

Spread love not hate

READ: MATTHEW 5:43–48

KEY VERSE V44
'But I tell you, love your enemies and pray for those who persecute you'

Do you know anyone who makes your life difficult? Perhaps it is people who keep telling you that your beliefs are childish and irrational and that faith in God is a waste of time. Whoever you consider an adversary, Jesus doesn't pull His punches here. He doesn't want us to merely tolerate our enemies; He wants us to love them! It won't be easy to love people who seem determined to undermine our faith and discredit our God, but this is what Jesus wants us to do. And by responding to their hostility with kindness, you're reflecting God's truth and goodness.

Maybe loving people we clash with and praying for them go together. Perhaps it's as we pray for them that God begins to show us how much He loves them. Maybe that process will begin to change us and will help us to love everyone as God does. This won't mean accepting everything arrogant people say, but it will mean being patient with them, keeping our temper under control and choosing to be a friend to them.

Pray
Spend some time praying for people who you don't have any easy relationship with. Pray for them by name, and ask Jesus to help you love each of these people, as He does.

HOT TOPIC | APOLOGETICS 2

**WEEKEND
18/19 AUG**

CREATION

Fine print

READ: PSALM 33:1–3

KEY VERSE V1
'Sing joyfully to the LORD, you righteous'

God is our creator. He created us in painstaking detail, making each of us unique. We all know that each of us has a unique set of fingerprints, but did you know that they were formed before you were even born? Their patterns grow with you as your hands and fingers continue to grow. They are just one of the amazing parts of the human body. Fingerprints are used as a form of identification and can even unlock your computer or smartphone. Knowing that God created us all as uniquely as this is surely worth a 'thank You' from us?

God sustains us too, keeping us going and giving us the good things we need day by day, such as unending love, hope for tomorrow and comfort in times of sadness. If that isn't enough, if we choose to follow Him, He recreates us, dealing with our sin and giving us a new life. God is an amazing creator – not just in how He put together the world around us, but in how He treats us too.

When we begin to fully grasp what God has done for us, it should make us feel good about ourselves, because it's obvious how much He loves us. Further on in Psalm 33 it says, 'He made their hearts, so he understands everything they do' (v15, NLT).

What God has done for us should inspire us to worship Him. We can respond with joy, and praise God for being so good to us. Over the next few days, we're going to look at a few verses from Psalm 33 in some detail. Our key verse today, verse 1, mentions singing – and that's a great way to worship, but it's not the only way. In everything we do and say, we can show God that we're grateful for how much He loves us and how much He's done for us.

Pray

Spend some time now thanking God for what He's done for you, and praising Him for being so amazing!

Worship your way

READ: PSALM 33:1–3

KEY VERSE VV2–3
'Praise the Lord with the harp... Sing to him a new song; play skilfully, and shout for joy.'

We mentioned yesterday that worshipping God doesn't just mean singing. So we shouldn't make the mistake of thinking that if we don't particularly like singing or can't play the harp (skilfully or not), we can't worship God. Singing worship songs is great, but anything we do can be an act of worship, if our attitude is right. What's more, when we get together to worship God, it's brilliant to do something new. The psalm says, 'Sing a new song'. Perhaps we could also say, 'Dance a new dance' or 'Paint a new painting'. Maybe there is another creative activity you enjoy, that could be a way to worship God.

When God made us, He made us to be just like Him. So, because He's amazingly creative, we can be creative too! We can use our God-given creativity to worship Him, and when we do, it brings a whole new dimension to our time with God. Worship becomes more exciting and vibrant for us – and, just maybe, it becomes more exciting for God, too! It would be very boring if we all worshipped the same way. There are so many ways in which we can express ourselves to God; just some of which include photography, dance, sculpture, poetry, even silence – oh, and music, of course!

Think

God has made you creative. How can you and your friends use that creativity to express yourselves to God? How can you do something new as you worship Him?

Share the love

READ: PSALM 33:3–5

KEY VERSE V5
'The Lᴏʀᴅ loves righteousness and justice; the earth is full of his unfailing love.'

God loves us! Hopefully you already know that. More than likely, you've heard people say that quite a few times. Often, just a quick look at the world around us and the good things in our lives confirms that God is with us, and that His love does, indeed, fill the earth! This might not always be obvious, however, particularly when we're suffering, but even then, God's promise holds true – He is always with us.

But there's a challenge coupled with that truth. If God is good and fair and loving, then we need to show that to other people. If we accept that God created us to be like Him, we should love justice, like He does. In fact, if we show God's love and justice to other people, this is part of our worship.

God loves it when we do something that's good and fair. Acting to help someone who feels left out or forgotten is a way for us to tell God that we think He's amazing – just as singing a worship song is.

➕ *Challenge*

Do something today to show someone that God loves them or to make sure that they are treated fairly. For example, go and do the washing up for your elderly neighbour, talk to the guy in your class or at college whom everyone else ignores, or give some of your money to charity.

CORE THEME | CREATION 3

Spread the news

READ: ACTS 4:8–22

KEY VERSE V20
'we cannot help speaking about what we have seen and heard.'

Going to a big live concert can be very exciting. Beforehand, you might find it difficult to think or talk about anything else. You plan your outfit, work out how you will get to the venue and count down the days until the actual event. Then afterwards you can't stop talking about it. When you've got a piece of news that's this good, you just can't keep it to yourself. You share it with your friends. But even more than sharing, you want other people to experience it for themselves.

Peter and John had seen and experienced that God was amazing. He'd done so much for them that they simply couldn't stop telling people about Him. Even when people tried to shut them up, they kept talking because they wanted everyone around them to hear about God and experience for themselves how good He is.

Our response should be the same. If we truly grasp how amazing, how creative and how surprising God is, and appreciate everything He has done for us, we won't be able to help telling people around us. And we'll not only want them to hear about God, we'll want them to get to know and experience Him for themselves.

Pray

Lord, You are amazing! Thank You for being so good to me and to the world. Help me to see more and more how amazing You are – and fire me up to tell other people about You. Amen.

CORE THEME | CREATION 3

God-filled heart

READ: ECCLESIASTES 3:9–13

KEY VERSE V11
'He has also set eternity in the human heart'

In our series on 'Creation', we've already taken a look at the incredible world around us and what it can tell us about the God who made it. To round it off, we'll think about God's plan for the people and the world He created. Why did God create us? How is God going to heal a suffering world? And how will all this end?

In today's reading, we find that an important part of God's plan for each of us is to know Him. Inside us all there's a longing for something lasting, something meaningful and eternal. We're designed to have our needs met by God in order to be fulfilled. Some people describe this as being born with a 'God-shaped hole' inside us. People try to fill this hole with all sorts of things: work, alcohol, romance, drugs, even family. The problem is none of these really fill the hole – they'll all leave us unsatisfied.

There's nothing wrong with enjoying life and having a good time. In fact, all the good things that make life enjoyable are gifts from God. But in the end, the only thing that will really satisfy us is a relationship with God. Anything else will ultimately let us down and leave us lacking. God created us to know Him – and we're not truly living until we do.

CORE THEME | CREATION 3

 ## Challenge

If you already know God, spend some time this weekend talking to Him, listening to Him and getting to know Him better.

Plans and purposes

READ: EPHESIANS 2:8–10

KEY VERSE V10
'He has created us anew in Christ Jesus, so we can do the good things he planned for us long ago.' (NLT)

The last two or three weeks of the summer term can sometimes seem a torture. Usually nothing fun or productive is done. Quite often, students just sit around, waiting for the holidays to start. Nobody wants to be there – including, probably, the teachers! When the final bell goes on the last day of term, the sense of relief and freedom can be huge. But, the funny thing is, within a week or two of being let out of school, some students can't wait to go back! Why? Because if there is nothing to do, they are desperately bored. They have no sense of purpose.

There's nothing more guaranteed to make you bored, frustrated and depressed than the feeling of having no purpose. Fortunately, we do have a purpose. God's plan for us is to do significant things that make a difference and which make earth more like heaven. God has created us to do good things. He's even planned out exactly what He wants each of us to do. God has an individual and unique purpose for each one of us. That is something to feel good about!

⬆ *Pray*

Lord God, thank You that You've given me a unique purpose in life. Please help me to understand more clearly what that purpose is and exactly how You want me to live it out. Amen.

Weekend

25/26 AUG

Best role model

READ: 1 JOHN 3:1–3

KEY VERSE V2
'But we know that when Christ appears, we shall be like him, for we shall see him as he is.'

Think back to when you were five years old. What did you enjoy? What did you want to be when you grew up? How wise were you at that point? Maybe you were an exception, but not many people are wise or mature when they're five! It's as we grow up that we become wiser, more mature and, we might say, a more complete version of ourselves. When we look back at how we used to be, we often laugh at how little we really knew.

We've already mentioned several times that God created us to be like Him. We're His children. But we're not exactly like Him. Because we make mistakes, because we don't yet understand God completely, we're imperfect. But John assures us that one day, when we see Jesus face to face, we will be exactly like Him. As we follow God, we grow up, get wiser and start to show more godly qualities; and, in the end, we will be like Him, as we were always meant to be. One day we'll be perfect. One day we'll be like Jesus. That's our destiny. That's God's plan for us.

 ## Challenge

One day we will be like Jesus. But that doesn't mean we get out of trying to be like Him in the meantime! Take an honest look at your lifestyle. Is there anything there that needs to change so that you can be more pure and more like Jesus?

Big surprise!

READ: 1 CORINTHIANS 2:7–10

KEY VERSE V9
'no mind has imagined what God has prepared for those who love him.' (NLT)

Can you remember your first Christmas? Not many people can! However, your parents will probably remember it very well. You may have had an expression of complete amazement all over your face. The presents, the cards, the decorations, the carols and the food were all completely new to you at that age. Of course now we take all these things a bit for granted but, at the time, these were new, surprising, amazing things. As a toddler, we could never have imagined what Christmas would be like until we experienced it.

These verses from 1 Corinthians tell us that, in the same way, it's impossible to imagine the wonderful things God has planned for us. As we follow Jesus, we get a few glimpses of what He has in mind, but we've seen nowhere near all of it yet! God's plan for the people He created is not just to save them from their sin; it's to overwhelm them with wonderful and amazing things. We may not see those things this side of heaven, but one day we will. As a heavenly parent, God must be looking forward to seeing our childlike amazement when we discover all that He has in store for us.

CORE THEME | CREATION 3

Pray
Thank God for His amazing plan and the wonderful things He has prepared for you.

God's builders

READ: MATTHEW 6:9–13

KEY VERSE V10
'your kingdom come, your will be done, on earth as it is in heaven.'

Have you ever watched the TV programme *Grand Designs*? Usually a couple have bought some land and have exciting ideas to build a brand-new building. The owners need to have imagination as to the end result because it starts off as just a patch of ground! Clearly this is a risk, but the owners can see their house gradually taking shape, bit by bit. The foundations are dug, the frame goes up, the walls and roof are added. Inside the plumbing, electrics and carpets are being arranged. The house that started as a plan on a piece of paper, finishes up as a physical building; the fulfilment of what the architect had planned. It is really exciting seeing it all coming together!

God is an architect. He has a plan and He's building something wonderful. He's already created a world that's beautiful, but He has a plan to build on it and make it perfect. God's plan is to make earth like heaven. But the truly amazing thing is that God chooses to use us as His builders. God could just do it all Himself, but He chooses to work with us to make earth like heaven. God, the architect, has a plan and, if we act according to that plan, we help Him to build something incredible.

Challenge

God wants us to work with Him to look after the planet. What could this mean for you? Campaigning against climate change? Or simply recycling more?

CORE THEME | CREATION 3

Together forever

READ: REVELATION 21:1–4

KEY VERSE V3

'God's home is now among his people! He will live with them, and they will be his people. God himself will be with them.' (NLT)

Yesterday, we thought about God's plan to make the earth perfect and the incredible privilege we have of playing a part in it. So, what happens when that part of God's plan is complete? These verses from Revelation answer that question. (Revelation is written in very symbolic language; let's not get too hung up on why the sea has disappeared or why Jerusalem is coming down out of the sky.)

For us, the important focus is in verses 3–4. Once God's plan for the world He created is complete, He will come and be with us. Not just in the sense we know now – that He's with us through the Holy Spirit – but rather He will be powerfully and permanently present with us to comfort us and get rid of anything that's imperfect. In this new perfect world, death, pain and suffering will not exist. So if we're suffering now as a consequence of the imperfect world and people around us, we can be comforted by the knowledge that this won't last forever. But if we're tempted to just sit back and wait for God's plan to happen, we should remember that, in the meantime, we each have a unique part to play in that plan.

Think

How does it make you feel to know that one day God will be with us and everything will be perfect? What can you do to play a part in God's plan in the meantime?

Spiritual exercise

READ: REVELATION 21:5–7

KEY VERSE 5
'I am making everything new!'

Do you like to keep yourself fit? Sometimes when we are either injured or too busy to exercise, it's alarming how quickly we get out of shape. After just a couple of weeks of inactivity, muscles can turn to mush, your heart and lungs can feel like they've clogged up and you generally feel a bit lethargic. Keeping your body in shape is hard work. It's comforting to know that in the end God will renew our sluggish, creaking bodies and make them perfect.

While we're waiting for God's plan for creation to be fulfilled, and for this perfect world to happen, there are a few things we should remember. The world around us was created by God. He holds everything together, and everything in creation points us towards God and reminds us how great He is. Also, God's given us responsibility for looking after creation, and the chance to play a part in His plan to make it perfect. God made all the people around us too. He loves each of us, and wants us to know Him and let Him recreate us and give us new life. It is a reminder not to get lazy but keep looking for ways in which we can keep active in our walk with God, until He returns and makes everything new.

 Think

How can you stay spiritually 'fit'? Is there something you could do every day to keep this in check?

CORE THEME | CREATION 3

Not the end!

READ: REVELATION 22:12–14

KEY VERSE V13
'I am the Alpha and the Omega, the First and the Last'

Alpha and Omega are the first and last letters of the Greek alphabet. Sometimes in ancient Greek art, the letters appear either side of Christ's head. When used symbolically in Christianity, they signify that God is the beginning and the end, meaning that God is eternal. The phrase 'alpha and omega' is mentioned three times in Revelation, perhaps to reinforce the message. Knowing that God has always existed and will always exist, brings great comfort and reassurance. Sometimes, life may seem unsettled and the future looks uncertain. But we know that whatever the future brings, our God will always be there with us. He created the world and us. He knows us inside and out. We are incredibly special to Him and He wants the best for us, today and forevermore.

We began our studies on 'Creation' at the very beginning. We're ending at the very end. And God is still creating! At the very start of the Bible, God creates. At the very end, God recreates. He makes everything new, and everyone who follows Him will share in the blessings that this renewed, perfected world brings. God was the creator in the beginning, He still is the creator, and He always will be.

CORE THEME | CREATION 3

Think

What have you learned from our readings on 'Creation'? What do you want to say to God about it all? What has challenged you? What will you do differently from now on?

ORDER FORM

4 EASY WAYS TO ORDER:

1. For credit/debit card payment, call 01252 784700 (Mon–Fri, 9.30am – 5pm)

2. Visit our online store at **www.cwr.org.uk/shop**

3. Send this form together with a cheque made payable to CWR to:
CWR, Waverley Abbey House, Waverley Lane, Farnham, Surrey GU9 8EP

4. Visit a Christian bookshop

YOUR DETAILS

Name:

CWR ID No. (if known):

Address:

Postcode:

Telephone No. (for queries):

Email:

SUBSCRIPTIONS (NON DIRECT DEBIT)	QTY	PRICE (INCLUDING P&P)			TOTAL
		UK	Europe	Elsewhere	
Mettle (1yr, 3 issues)		£14.75	£17.60	£18.75	
				TOTAL	

. Please circle which four-month issue you would like your subscription to commence from:

Jan–Apr **May–Aug** **Sep–Dec**

Order direct from CWR or from your National Distributor. For a full list of our National Distributors and contact details, visit **www.cwr.org.uk/distributors**

Mettle is also available as a Digital Edition. For more information visit **www.mettleapp.org.uk**